Management Lessons of Vyasa for Sustainable Growth
Reference to the Indian Epics

Dr. Veda D Malagatti

Ukiyoto Publishing

All global publishing rights are held by

Ukiyoto Publishing

Published in 2023

Content Copyright © Dr. Veda D Malagatti

ISBN 9789359202679

All rights reserved.
No part of this publication may be reproduced, transmitted, or stored in a retrieval system, in any form by any means, electronic, mechanical, photocopying, recording or otherwise, without the prior permission of the publisher.

The moral rights of the author have been asserted.

This book is sold subject to the condition that it shall not by way of trade or otherwise, be lent, resold, hired out or otherwise circulated, without the publisher's prior consent, in any form of binding or cover other than that in which it is published.

www.ukiyoto.com

Dedication

I profusely thank all those who supported me during the writing of this book. The present work is the result of the guidance, co-operation, and support that I have received from a number of noble hearts of all contributors directly and indirectly for their untiring persistence, co-operation and inspiration. I also owe a lot to my benevolent professor Dr.A.H.Chacadi, my research guide: formor dean and director of Kousali Institute of Management Studies, Karnatak University, Dharwad, Karnataka State, India and emeritus professor of Chetan Business School, Hubballi, Karnataka State, India. I'm also indebted to Dr.Mukund Dixit, formor IIM-A professor, Karnataka state, India and Dr.Anupama Malagi, RV Institute of Management Studies, Bengaluru, India. We dedicate this book to my family, my father and my brother who motivated me for completing this book and supported me in my household chores which may prove dictionary of life to those who practise research with passion, students and hope it prove to be beam of light in their professional life.

Preface

The study clearly reveals that Vedas and Upanishads are the sources of both spiritual knowledge and science and technology of the world. Values of Hindu culture and tradition is based on Bhagavad-Gita and many Indian epics that energize common people to do genuine effort to build the character of good and wise man in order to reach the destination of spiritual life. Art and Science of Management studies indulge use of skills which are already mentioned in the Bhagwad Gita. Skills like analyzing, interpreting situation, teamwork and working in integration are already practiced in Vyasa which is just a literature. Evolution of different analogies has created different branches of studies. In management studies itself there are different specializations but the above Vyasa mentioned are the common plethora among these specializations. The Metaphor of this has created essentiality of building skills but these are already mentioned in our vyasa and we are unaware of it. Even such vyasa inspire and motivates us in the similar senses.

This is totally based on the secondary data. Various books referred is mentioned in the references. Being a budding author in this management studies, the chapters and the verses mentioned in Bhagwad Gita is being abstracted as it is. Globally, this has resulted in the decline of the physical, mental and spiritual health of individuals, discrimination and everyday crimes in the society, endless wars between the nations and destruction of mother earth. Ancient Gurukul inherited wisdom to greater extent though there was austerity of amenity. The Universal Concept of manager endeavors dynamic, excellent, who are passionate and innovative in crafting their own solutions to business problems. MBA education or Management equips you to be a good and competent Manager. Every Company needs a manager in order to manage resources, people, projects and funds. MBA is capable of transforming students and working professionals into Competent Managers who are responsible and capable enough to handle and sort out any problems which hamper or affect the working of their company. There will be managerial effectiveness and efficiency if these management lessons which are mentioned in the book are used @ 60% in our daily practice.

Contents

Introduction	1
Insights Of Intellectual Expendition Mentioned In Ancient Vyasa	3
Management Framework For Observing Corporate Practise	18
Management Lessons For Life Skills:	33
Whose Lessons Is The Best? Arjuna Or Hanuman Or Ravanna	47
Life Skills For Ethical Sustainable Life	57
About the Author	*63*

Introduction

Using the qualitative method of study, the wider application of Upanishads lessons and teaching of Bhagavad-Gita application has been discussed with reference to scientific discoveries, technological innovation and diffusion, socio-cultural development and religious purification. The study clearly reveals that Vedas and Upanishads are the sources of both spiritual knowledge and science and technology of the world. Upanishads teach to human being that all life forms move through repeated cycles of birth, death, and rebirth, until final liberation from this cycle, Moksha to bring people out from the mode of ignorance. Values of Hindu culture and tradition which is based on Bhagavad- Gita, energize common people to do genuine effort to build the good character to reach their final destination of success in career too by. Indian Epics (Vyasa) was devastating as war in its plain sense, though initially keeping to chivalrous notions of warfare, both sides soon began adopting disreputable tactics to survice. At the end of the ferocious 18-day battle, though the Pandavas and Krishna managed to survive, it was not a victory for them, for the war had created the emptiness in their life by abandoning the true essence of life and the victory tainted the rest of their lives. These Vyasas have already mention the Good and Bad lessons of life. Vedas (Singh,2017), globally, has resulted in the drastically decline the physical, mental and spiritual health of individuals leading to discrimination and everyday crimes in the society, endless wars between the nations and destruction of mother earth. Vedas have been misinterpreted by self-proclaimed foreign Vedic scholars to subjugate Hinduism by catalyzing it with modern western theories and proclaiming new concepts of Management Lessons.

Ancient Gurukul inherited wisdom to greater extent though there was austerity of amenity. Wisdom does not consist in gathering information but consists in finding a clear access to the highest. In other words, Wisdom enshrouds the vision of ignorance. Knowledge is the highest security which destroys anguish, it destroys doubt, it destroys [weakness; and makes it more productive. Our first duty is to God to practice holiness by gaining excellent knowledge. The one who lacks in resolution and tranquility, in vain does he seek knowledge. God provided Bliss of higher vision—Humility, Unostentatiousness, Non-injuring, Forgiveness, Simplicity, Purity, Steadfastness, Self-Control; this is declared to be wisdom. The Universal Concept of manager endeavors dynamic, excellent, who are passionate and innovative in crafting their own solutions to business problems. MBA equips you to be a good and competent Manager. Every Company needs a manager in order to manage resources, people, projects and funds. MBA is capable of transforming students and working professionals into Competent Managers who are responsible and capable enough to handle personal life effectively and sort out any problems which hamper or affect the working of their company. These Management lessons emphasizes on type of skills building to be competent in this dynamic world which is already embossed by our Vyasa (Indian Epic).

Insights Of Intellectual Expendition Mentioned In Ancient Vyasa

1.1 Gitopanishads:

A body of Ancient Knowledge base The Bhagavad-Gita technically belongs to the smrti literature that indicates that it is authoritative and needs heed to be heard and is often called Gitopanishad. However, since it is considered as the utterance of the incarnated God Lord Krishna himself, the Bhagavad-Gita is approved as a part shruti *(heard/revealed: Vedas and Upanishads)* and is often called Gitopanishad which reflects all human wisdom and knowledge. Human beings often stood perplexed and mystified as they confronted paradoxical situations in life that demanded action. The Bhagavad-Gita is an intelligent response to a perennial human predicament to resolve in their own way by discerning right from wrong. In Bhagavad Gita, the epic of Mahabharath, Lord Krishna outlines the Pandava prince Arjuna, for him the path towards gaining flawless self-knowledge and self-mastery from his sorrowful state of confusion standing in the mid of Kurukshetra (a battle between the Pandavas and Kauravas) and opened his eyes to perceive the truths beyond appearances around him dispassionately with an attitude of detachment. Lord Krishna, the supreme Guru, tutors his confused disciple, Arjuna, to lead him from the state of maya (illusion) to the perfect understanding of satyasyasatyam (really real).

The **Bhagavad-Gita** presents Arjuna as an embodiment of the human predicament worthy of deepest reverence. The Bhagavad-Gita was written to lead Arjuna from the slavery and obscurity of avidya (ignorance) to the freedom and splendor of jnana (wisdom). Moksha (liberation/enlightenment) is the purging of the illusory thoughts thus entering a state of pure consciousness and realising and accepting reality as it is. Pure consciousness is in a state of samadhi (equanimity), being in control of one's mind and body. Impure consciousness is a state of being blinded and disturbed by the ego. In the last section of the Bhagavad-Gita (18:66), the Lord Krishna reiterates sarva-dharmanparityajya, mam ekamsaranamvraja, ahamtvamsarva-papebhyo, mokshayisyami ma *suchah*. (Abandon all religions [beliefs and concepts] and take recourse of God to liberate from all sins. Do not be afraid.) Many people such as Mahatma Gandhi found solace in this Celestial Song: The main purpose of Vedas is to find the ultimate goal of life (self-realization through Karma so that it is not meant for the creation of armchair speculators but for the formation of character as the power to analyze existing materials, prakriti (nature) and Purusha (supremepower) in the proper perspective. Thus, one must deliver him/herself with the help of his/her mind to never ever degrade himself/herself. When doubts or disappointment haunts then Bhagwad-Gita is one ray of hope on the horizon. Those who meditate on the Gita will derive fresh joy and new meanings from it every day as each chapter is envisioned as a kind of *yoga* in itself and the function of *yoga* is to train our body and mind until it reaches *samadhi* (equanimity/liberation/enlightenment).

According to the *Gita*, 18 chapters contain imbibing every aspect of our life which are salutary alongwith those aspects that seem negative and these chapters have a progressive order to their teachings of the system of yogas also. Below mentioned different types of yogas are only steppingstones on the path of creating consciousness, one who knows everything in fully namely the Absolute truth, the living entities, the material nature and their manifestations with paraphernalia:

- Chapter 1: *Vishada yoga* is the yoga of the dejection). When Arjuna sees his near and dear ones on the opposing army side of the Kurus, he loses morale and objects, obviously one can't hurt the dear ones basically along with the fears of the sinful apprehensions of killing. This lesson teaches us to overcome the feeling of rejection and uphold one-shelf with ignorance and determinant to rise.

- Chapter 2: *Samkhya Yoga* is the yoga of knowledge. Krishna begins countering Arjuna's objections with logical reasoning explaining the three principles *dharma*, (right action) *atman* (individual self) and *sarira* (body) and explains him that as a warrior, his duty is to uphold the path of *dharma* as the eternal self is immortal. Duty conscious is utmost superior as it is accountable to your atma. Our duty is to just go on enhancing our knowledge and apply it in working environment.

- Chapter 3: *Karma Yoga* is the yoga of action. Arjuna questions why he should engage in fighting if knowledge is more important than action. Krishna then explains *nishkama karma* (performing one's duties without desiring its fruits - detached activity) as the appropriate course of action (3:3-8). He explains that both improper action and neglect of duty are impelled by lack of knowledge. One should go on performing without any expectations in return.

- Chapter 4: *Jnana-Karma-Sanyasa Yoga* is the yoga of knowledge, discipline of action and knowledge. Krishna reveals to Arjuna that his incarnations are created for the defence of the virtuous and the destruction of the wicked (4:7). Krishna glorifying transcendental knowledge and appeals to Arjuna to arm himself with this knowledge to burn the evil effects.

- Chapter 5: *Karma-Sanyasa Yoga* is the yoga of action and knowledge. Arjuna wants to know if it is better to renounce action or to be involved in action (5:1). The action of silence when there is lot of ambiguities is the feasible solutions to take the ultimate decisions. The wise person can understand a position to see action in inaction and inaction in action.

- Chapter 6: *Dhyana Yoga*, or *Atmasamyama Yoga* explains the correct posture for meditation towards the Samadhi which enriches the concentration level and focus on how to achieve it.

- Chapter 7: *Jnana-Vijnana Yoga* is the yoga of knowledge of Nirguna Brahma and manifest divinity. Krishna instructs the path of knowledge *(Jnana Yoga)*. *There is strong positive correlation between the knowledge and the karma.*

- Chapter 8: *Akshara-Brahma Yoga* is the yoga of indestructible Brahma. This yoga teaches us how one can attain his supreme abode while one is on the bed of death. This pinpoints that devotion practice will decide the easiest way to attain liberation (Moksha).

- Chapter 9: *Raja-Vidya-Raja-Guhya Yoga* - This Yoga reveals one-self, although independent and aloof which pervades creates and annihilates own cosmos energy. This awareness is recommended as a way to remember him in all circumstances. God is the sovereign science and the sovereign secret that compensates for the deficiencies of devotee, take care of devotees and preserve their strength and in return he expects just a offering of a leaf, a flower, or some water with devotion. Even if a devotee unintentionally commits a dreadful sin God still promises for his well-being.

- Chapter 10: *Vibhuti-Vistara-Yoga* is the yoga of divine glories. Krishna explains his grandeur more specifically and thereby reveals himself as one of the Supreme Personality of Godhead - the source of all sages, the source of the material and spiritual worlds that is the source of inheriting all qualities and attitudes.

- Chapter 11: *Visvarupa-Darsana Yoga* is a yoga of the vision of the universal form. God displays his *visvarupa* (universal form) which is imbibed with a theophany emitting the radiance of a thousand suns, containing all beings and substances in existence of expansive form. Universal Vision is the foundation element of our Karma and Dharma.

- Chapter 12: *Bhakti Yoga* describes the benefits of devotion. Devotion to worship Krishna (incarnate God) through devotional service or the impersonal God (Ningana Brahma). He also explains different forms of devotions and spiritual disciplines. One who is engaged in active service of devotion will definitely seek the Absolute opulence.

- Chapter 13: *Kshetra-KshetrajnaVibhaga Yoga* is the yoga of discrimination between the field and the knower of the field. Krishna describes the human body as *kshetra* (temple/field), stating that one who knows this fact is a *kshetrajna* (knower). Krishna describes *prakrti* (nature/matter), the *purusha* (enjoyer/spirit) and consciousness. Unassumingly advancing in knowledge, one can become free from worldly entanglement. We are the actors in this world acting our respective roles till we are breathing on this earth.

- Chapter 14: *Gunatraya-Vibhaga Yoga* classifies our behavior into three *gunas* or *traits* of material nature, namely *satvaguna*, *rajoguna* and *tamoguna* (goodness, passion and ignorance), respectively. These three forces control all conditioned persons within this world. A discerning person is of *satva* nature. It is possible to transcend the bondages of these *gunas* through devotion. When enlightened by pious activities, they approach Supreme Lord in different capacities – as the distressed, desire of money, the inquisitive, and those in search of knowledge. Supreme God is the controller of the individual's soul, the body and these Gunas of character.

- Chapter 15: *Purusottama Yoga* is the yoga of the supreme person. It explains the ways and means to free oneself from the grip of the three *gunas* of matter. Krishna invites Arjuna to fell this tree with the "axe of detachment", in order to progress towards his supreme abode.

• Chapter 16: *Daivasura-Sampad-Vibhaga Yoga* is about the realization of discrimination between the divine and the demonical properties). Krishna indicates the divine and the demonic traits present in human nature. He further explains that after twenty-six godly qualities, the demoniac nature which degrades the soul through arrogant, ignorant, and conceited pursuits the sense of gratification and power. He counsels that, in order to attain the supreme destination which is salvation than one must give up lust, anger and greed. By assistance by *buddhi* (intellect), supported by scriptural confirmation, one is able to discern right and wrong and act appropriately.

• Chapter 17: *Sraddhatraya-Vibhaga Yoga* is the classification of the threefold faith. Krishna mentions three divisions of beliefs, thoughts, deeds and even eating habits corresponding to the three *gunas* mentioned above in chapter 14.

• Chapter 18: *Moksha-Sanyasa Yoga* is about self-surrender and liberation through the path of knowledge. It is a review of the truths already presented. In conclusion, Krishna advises Arjuna to abandon all forms of *dharma* and simply surrender unto him (18:66). He describes this as the ultimate perfection of life. After listening to the instructions of Sri Krishna, Arjuna listens to Sri Krishna who is the master of all mystics with enormous admiration, surrenders himself to take the next step is considers confirmed and gets ready to fight.

1.2 Touch of Divinity and Mystique leads to Spirituality

The Gita advises to perform action with loving attention to the Divine which implies redirection of the empirical self away from its egocentric needs, desires, and passions for creating suitable conditions to perform actions in pursuit of excellence. Tagore says working for love is freedom in action which is described as disinterested work in accordance to the Gita. It is on the basis of the holistic vision that Indians have developed the work-ethos of life. They found that all work irrespective of its nature have to be directed towards a single purpose that is the manifestation of essential divinity in man by working for the good of all beings - lokasangraha. This vision was presented to us in the very first mantra of Isopanishad which says that whatever exists in the Universe is enveloped by God. How shall we enjoy this life then, if all are one? The answer it provides is enjoy and strengthen life by sacrificing your selfishness by not coveting other's wealth. The same motivation is given by Sri Krishna in the Third Chapter of Gita when He says that 'He who shares the wealth generated only after serving the people, through work done as a sacrifice for them, is freed from all the sins. On the contrary those who earn wealth only for themselves, eat sins that lead to frustration and failure. The *Bhagavad-Gita* is thoroughly practical and free of any intellectual gymnastics, or vague, abstract philosophy. It offers diagnostic solutions to every challenging situation that we face in our daily life that calls for discernment and action. The *Bhagavad-Gita* is thoroughly practical and free of any intellectual gymnastics, or vague, abstract philosophy. Gita is not rigid and offers diagnostic solutions to every challenging situation that we face in our daily life that calls for discernment and action. Above that Panchajanya (five victories) points to the spiritual victory of Aum over the five elements (*bhutas*), mastery over the five bodies (*koshas*) and control over the five sense organs (*indriyas*) are highly recommendable. Devadatta (God-given) proclaims Aum as the key to liberation given by God himself to human beings. Paundra (mighty sound) announces Aum as the supreme Word of Power. Anantavijaya (unending victory) states the effect of the recitation (*japa*) of Aum. Sughosha (great/excellent sound) makes known the ecstatic experience of those who recite Aum. Manipushpaka (could mean jewelled bracelet, flowery mind, aerial chariot of the mind, and so on). Through the recitation of Aum, the mind is transformed into a precious jewel. At the recitation of Aum the mind blossoms like a flower. Aum causes the mind to open up and soar in the *Chidakasha* (sky of consciousness). Apart from chanting, the sounding of the conchs thus symbolically portrays the yogi, engaged in the interior battle, who has brought under control all his faculties in meditation and united them in the constant invocation of Aum, causing it to vibrate throughout his being. By its continual intonation, Aum resounds throughout the "sky" (mind) and "earth" (body) of the yogi, and bursts apart the hearts of all the foes of the self, for the consciousness arising from its invocation first to render powerless, and then annihilates them (1:19).

Now, one should ponder carefully as it is learned that wisdom is the secret of secrets. Then act as you think best. No coercion, no promises, no threats. It is up to the listener to decide. The *Gita* simply shows us the way forward. Some people insist that Sacred Scriptures can have only one meaning and, therefore, eschew interpretations and even translations (Frein 2012:12). However, this is a mistaken assumption with regard to the Hindu Sacred Scriptures in Sanskrit. Hindu scriptures are intended to have multi-level messages and subtle nuances. Their literary style (sutras and *shlokas*: aphorisms and versifications) demands, necessitates, and provides room for any number of commentaries and interpretations. Words that carry several relevant ideas are ideal for the profound wisdom of the *Gita* and the Upanishads, in particular. The Hindu scriptures consist of unlimited layers, many symbolic in nature (Knapp 2012). In addition, the meanings of the symbols are not fixed. They may change according to the level on which they occur. Body is the chariot, soul the traveler, intellect the charioteer, mind the bridle, five senses are five horses, while desires are the paths on which those horses gallop. (*Kathopanishad* 1:3:3, 4).

1.3   Arouse the Senses of Dwell for Opulence of Pious:

Krishna (literally, the dark one) and Arjuna (literally, the white one) represent the unknown and the known (God and human person), as well as our own dual nature as immortal and mortal. From this standpoint, the dialogue between Krishna and Arjuna can be regarded both as God's communication to human beings and the communication of our own divine Self with our human self, the intention of which is *moksha/samadhi* or liberation from sufferings (equanimity). Accordingly, Arjuna and Krishna are the indwelling *atman* (individual self) and *Paramatman* (immortal self) riding the chariot, which is Arjuna's body. The *Mundakopanishad* speaks of two birds of golden plumage; inseparable companions, the individual self and the immortal self, as perched on the branches of the same tree. The former tastes of the sweet and bitter fruits of the tree, whereas the latter, tasting of neither, calmly observes. The individual self, deluded by forgetfulness of its identity with the divine self, bewildered by its ego, grieves and is sad. However, when it recognizes *Paramatman* as its own true self, and beholds its glory, it grieves no more *Mundakopanishad*. These verses are a perfect summary of the *Gita*. Arjuna is the bewildered and sorrowing *atman*, the individual self, and Krishna is the divine *Paramatman*, the supreme self from which the *atman* derives its very being and existence. Forgetful of its true nature as part of the cosmic/universal/immortal self, the finite *atman* passes through countless experiences producing utterly false conclusions that compounds and perpetuates the illusion and sorrow. Only when the perspective of the divine self is entered into, will its plight fade away. The next item is being engaged in the cultivation of knowledge and it is duty of the Sanyasi to distribute knowledge to the forgotten. For Salvation, Sanyasi is supposed to beg from door to door for their livelihood and it does not mean that they are beggar. Such humility is the qualification of a transcendental stage towards advancement of mastering the spirituality and one should not construe for their own personal interest.

Bhagavad Gita discusses in great details the theory of cause and effect, making the doer responsible for the consequences of his deeds. The Gita, while advising detachment from the avarice of selfish gains by discharging one's accepted duty, does not absolve anybody of the consequences arising from discharge of his responsibilities. Thus the best means for effective work performance is to become the work itself. Attaining this state of nishkama karma is the right attitude to work because it prevents the ego, the mind from dissipation through speculation on future gains or losses. Intrigue and Curiosity goes hand and hand. One should be intrigue towards the persistence work. Curiosity elites enthusiasm to learn better with prudence and perservance too. For enthusiasm, alertness in 360 degree angle is very crucial. Listening skill too is the basic need of an hour and this skill aids in seeking all type of information from everyone surrounding you. Listening to someone carefully creates belongingness. Inadequate listening will refrain one from leading.

Dwelling about God purifies a person who constantly engages in listening to the eternal language and music. By such development of devotional service one becomes freed from the modes of passion and ignorance and thus material lust and avarice are diminished with wiping off the impurities. A person remains steady in his position of pure goodness, becomes enlivened and understands the science of God perfectly. Science of God's cores excludes these eight comprises of Earth, water, fire, air, ether, intelligence and false ego.

Lord Shree Krishna in his verse, lists the things that disturb one's peace, and then asks to give them up:

1.   **Material desires** - Either way, we get trapped. A harbor of desire is a trap of greed and anger. So the path to inner peace does not lie in fulfilling desires, but instead by not providing the scope for it.

2.   **Greed** - Firstly, chase for material advancement is an endless one and great waste of time. In developed countries, their hankering is still unsatisfied though very few people are deprived of enough to eat and wear. Thus, those who possess the contentment for wealth of divinity possess one of the biggest treasures of life.

3.   **Ego** - Mark H McCormack, author of "What they don't teach you at Harvard Business School"; writes: "Most corporate executives are one giant ego, with a couple of arms and legs sticking out." Statistics reveal that a majority of executives, who lose their jobs in the senior management level, do so not because of professional incompetence, but because of interpersonal issues that erupts stems from the ego. The way to peace is not to nurture and increase pride, but to get rid of it.

4.   **Proprietorship / Ownership-** The feeling of proprietorship is based upon ignorance because the whole world belongs to God. We came empty-handed in the world, and we will go back empty-handed. We can't think of worldly things as ours but take up the ownership of our role authorized in this earthly world.

Gita further explains the import of theory of non- attachment to the results of work in Ch.18 that the entire credit should not be appropriated by the doer alone. If the result of sincere effort whether it is a failure or success, the entire blame does not accrue to the doer. The former attitude of success mollifies arrogance and conceit while the feeling of failure prevents excessive despondency, de-motivation and self-pity. Thus both these dispositions safeguard the doer against psychological vulnerability which is the cause for the Modem Managers' health companions like Diabetes, High B.P. Ulcers etc. One of the main reasons for non-attachment to results is because workings of the world are not designed to positively respond to our calculations and hence expected fruits may not always be forthcoming. One of the attributes of attitude is preserved with ego than it meteorites the righteousness. Blind Dhritarashtra of Mahabharata is the false self, blinding everyone to adhere to everything essence of hatred in very crooked manner because that instinct was deep rooted within there in on the throne of his body and mind, awaiting for the recapturing of its rightful kingdom. Duryodhana (dirty fighter), the elder son of Dhritarashtra (one who holds the kingdom), is a dangerous evolution of his blind father since he is no longer blind, yet he is capable of consciously choosing evil if he believes that it serves his ambition. He is coercing the virtuous to commit self-sacrifice in order to gratify his hunger for power. This shows that the virtuous person serving the ego and working to ensure its preservation are certainly risking their lives. It is amazing to note how the ego devours virtuous people, sapping their energy, turning them into blind brutes, still believing that they are really living a great life. This is the fatal delusion in which human beings often dwell from the glimpses of the truth of their inner divinity. The ideas mentioned above have a close bearing on the end-state of a manager which is his mental health. Sound mental health is the very goal of any human activity more so management. An expert describes sound mental health as that state of mind which can maintain a calm, positive poise or regain it when unsettled in the midst of all the external vagaries of work life and social existence. Internal constancy and peace are the pre- requisites for a healthy stress-free mind for further scope of exploration. We say that time is the healer but the extent of it's healing differ from person to person. It depends on their gratification of strength and power to digest the odds.

Individuals are categorized in two categories as under:

Unfortunate persons are mentioned in Vyasa as under:

Less intelligent persons, bereft of devotional service, cannot understand the Lord's activities, and therefore such persons describe these activities as imaginatory/hallucination effect and consider God to be non-existence and are determined to be arrogant.

1) The living entity is āśraya, always subordinate, and the Supreme Personality of Godhead is viṣaya, the supreme objective, the goal of life. A person in asraya are those who acts madly lust and haunted by his real business so that he can enjoy so-called happiness in the bodily concept of life and want to be promoted to the heavenly planets to achieve fortunate positions. Pure devotees of the Lord are not at all interested in such opulence.

2) Being attached to the miserable material conditions, a materialistic person try to get some sense of gratification engaged in maintaining the body and self with dresses, ornaments, garlands and ointments.

3) Persons who are bereft of the all-auspicious performance of chanting are also bereft of good sense. When invited to attend a meeting of devotees, they suddenly become reluctant.

4) Unfortunate people, even after hearing all the evidence of Vedic literature from great personalities, still have no faith in God

Fortunate persons are mentioned in Vyasa as under:

1) Deluded by the three modes of virtuous - goodness, passion and ignorance

2) Pious men render devotional service unto God who is searching for knowledge of the Absolute and work for more of philanthropy activity.

3) Of these, the wise one is in full knowledge. Such people preach Morality and practice these principles of life.

4) All these devotees are undoubtedly magnanimous soulsto dwell the transcendental service.

1.4 Requisition To Act - Both In Divine And Human:

Krishna reminds Arjuna of his obligation to act:

Surely none can ever remain inactive even for a moment; for everyone is helplessly driven to action by nature-born qualities. He who outwardly restraining the organs of sense and action, sits mentally dwelling on the objects of senses, that man of deluded intellect is called a hypocrite. However, Krishna points towards the possibility of acting without any attachment, which is sacrifice (3:9). Krishna points towards God as the best example for this kind of "perfect action". According to Krishna, God's creative activity in itself was a sacrifice. Arjuna is made to understand that every act of the Creator is a sacrifice. The world has originated, is sustained and supported through sacrifice. Our vocation as human beings is to collaborate consciously and actively in this ongoing divine sacrifice. Feed gods and get fed by gods - be a conscious collaborator in this eternal feeding-chain. Krishna calls those who refuse to engage in self-sacrificing activities, thieves (3:12). Acting with a desire for its fruit is a disgraceful act like a cow that drinks its own milk. It already had its share of milk as a calf and now her milk is for her calf. Krishna demands from Arjuna action without attachment, seeking only the maintenance of the world order (3:25).

The *Mahabharata,* often known as the Hindu bible, is the story of a great war. It is one of the two Sanskrit epic poems of ancient India (the other being the Ramayana). The poem is made up of nearly 100000 couplets (approximately seven times the length of the *Iliad* and the *Odyssey* combined or 12 times the length of the Bible) or approximately 1.8 million words in total. Its authorship is traditionally ascribed to the sage Vyasa, although it is unlikely that a single person wrote the poem (Chaturvedi 2006:24). The author Vyasa himself appears in the work as the grandfather of the Kauravas and the Pandavas. The *Mahabharata* not only displays a riveting plot and a compelling dramatic structure, but is also full of wisdom. Its characters are complex and real, with depth of personality that is unmatched in any other story humanity has ever conceived. The *Mahabharata* contains numerous mythological and didactic material arranged around a central heroic narrative that tells of the struggle for sovereignty between the Kauravas and the Pandavas. The traditional date for the war that is the central event of the *Mahabharata* is 1302 BCE, but most historians assign it a later date. The best scholarly evidence indicates that the earliest layers of the epic were composed between 2500 and 3000 years ago. The oldest preserved parts of the text are not thought to be appreciably older than 400 BCE, although the origins of the story probably fall between the 8th and the 9th centuries BCE. The text reached its present form by 300-400 CE. According to the *Mahabharata* itself, the tale is an extended text from a shorter version of 24000 verses called simply *Bharata*. The present poem is divided into 18 books or *parvas*.

1.5 Simple Skills Recommended Based On Vyasa But Difficult To Practice:

1)   An intentional learning for transformation:

For this you require self-analysis. It has immediate effect on the brain. Habit needs to be disciplined acts like a transmitter which shows that a single day workout can improve your ability to shift and focus attention and that focus improvement will last for at least few days. Such actions increases concentration and it positively will influence one's reactions. Habit to be disciplined is created by long-term practice. Looking at effects of long-term practice is improved attention function dependent on your kind of regularity. One not only gets better focus and attention, but the volume of the hippocampus – which is a core centre of lateral ventricle of the brain that controls thoughts, emotion, memory, and the autonomic nervous system increases as well. The most transformative thing that regular exercise will do is its protective effects on brain. Here one can think brain like a muscle, the more one is working out, the bigger and stronger is its effect. Why is it important? Because brain and heart are the two areas that are most susceptible to get ill-effected and normal cognitive learning process effects. So with increased practice over your lifetime, you are not going to cure disease of arrogant, aggressive, and rebellion but what you are going to do is you are going to create the strongest hippocampus so it takes longer time for these diseases to actually have an effect. Good news is that you don't have to become a triathlete to get these results. The rule of thumb is bringing exercise/practice in your life will not only keep you happier, more protective life today, but it will protect your brain from incurable diseases. In his way it will change the trajectory of your life for the better.

2) Creating Synergy by Always Smiling:

Begin your day and your day with a Smile, your life will be sweet and feel likeheaven.One should get up with a smile and smile while sleeping. If you don't smile than they say whole day will be ill-effected and it is not because of day but due to attitude of a person. If your heart is not good than how can you expect the world to be happy with you? We say this is kalyuga, and it is due to dharma & karma of manusa(human being). There are classification of yugas created due to changes in the attitude, dharma and karma of human being. If you oblige satya then it will be satyayuga. Bit of hardship in thraytha yoga, charity/donations is dyaparayuga, if you earn and share is kalyuga. This radiance effects the brain and relaxes the body. Sun says I always emit rays of brightness and radiance since from so many 450crs years. Under rays, same fruits ripen, the natural biotic elements air, river, trees, mountains, sky, etc., existed since from so many years. Humans are creator of yuga and satyayuga is the requisition of today's era. Mind and heart changes as per mood swings but nature will never. Beautiful Day and good gestures are controllable by humans. If our vision is good than whole day and world is good and one should always attempt to have such good vision.

3) Change to Intentional Growth:

People tend to get into ruts in life and they don't try to break out of it even when it is taking them in the wrong direction. If you want to reach your potential and become the person you were created to be, you must do much more than just experience life and go out of your way to seize growth opportunities. For that you have to train your brain every day or every night before going to sleep about the strategies of your growth. For this you have one or more mistaken beliefs creating gaps that keep you from growing and reaching your potential. One has to look at these misconceptions that may be holding your growth:

a) The Assumption Gap: No one improves by accident. Personal growth doesn't happen on its own but one has to realize that one must take ownership of the growth process. To improve our life, our conscious goal should be to improve ourself by simply living.

b) The Knowledge Gap: You decide where you need or want to grow, you choose what you want to learn and you follow the discipline going at the pace you set. A lesson to work smartly is possible by hard efforts, consistency with discipline and learning to work differently. Even the cracks on the door of your personal door should be seen as opportunity.

c) The Timing Gap: When one is able to identify that there is a problem or likely to be one soon than one has to become alert. Whenever you think that there is a minute crack than there should not be scope to widen it and immediately it should attended and resolved.

d) The Mistake Gap: Warren Bennis asserts, "A mistake is simplyanother way of doing things" One should welcome mistake as a learning lesson of life and take a move in the right direction.

e) GROW FROM INSIDE: One has to control the desires beyond. We has to

i) Earn more than you spend.

ii) Spend less within your earning. Learn the smartness to spend with any financial commitments like credit, loans or any liability.

iii) One has to build the Good character with good intentions and virtues. The words that reaches the heart trains the brain. So one should be very careful with your actions too. Personality traits should be controlled with wisdom otherwise it is a great destruction of life.

iv) Respect and Observe all type of relationship. Never allow to depart anyone from your life.Growth never comes quickly or climbs to the top easily. People need to create and here is the formula: Preparation (growth) + Attitude + Opportunity +Action (performing with improvement) = Luck. One cannot change their destination but can change the direction to fulfill the potentiality for personal growth with good character. Character Growth determines the height of your personal Growth.

Management Framework For Observing Corporate Practise

2.1 Understanding Corporate Life

A) Concept of Organization

In Corporate the design of organization is the backbone of management and also imperial because without an efficient organization management cannot perform its functions smoothly. These functions in the business are to accomplish pre-determined goals. Organization has a structural framework of duties and responsibilities required of personnel in performing various functions with a view to achieve business goals. Louis Allen specified organization as the process of identifying and grouping the work to be performed enabling people to work together effectively in accomplishing objectives. Wheeler states that Functional framework within organization is well structural framework of duties and responsibilities of personnel and essentially a blue print of actions of performance resulting in a mechanism for carrying out function both vertically and horizontally to achieve the goals set-up by company management. Koontz and O'Donnell say organization establishes the authority relationships for co-ordination between personnel. Spriegel, in its broadest sense refers to various factors organization meant for endeavor of the relationship between the various factors present in a given endeavor. Factory organization concerns itself primarily with the internal relationships within the factory such as responsibilities of personnel, arrangement and grouping of machines and material control.

The essential and important elements of a good organization are as follows:

Element # 1. **It Must be Helpful in the Achievement of Objectives,**

Element # 2. There Must be Harmonious Grouping of Functions,

Element # 3. An Organization Must be Complete in All Respect,

Element # 4. There must be Perfect Co-Ordination in All the Activities of an Organisation,

Element # 5. There Must be Reasonable Span of Control,

Element # 6. Proper Utilization of Resources be Made,

Element # 7. Provision of Expansion,

Element # 8. Employees Satisfaction is Essential,

Element # 9. Policy be Such Which Can be Executed Easily and Economically.

B) Motivation and conflict resolution Theories:

Motivation theories help management teams determine the best way to achieve a business goal or work toward a desired outcome. The critical question in every Manager's mind is how to be effective in his job. Bhagavad Gita suggests 'one should always try to manage oneself'. For this every employee's opinion and suggestions should be anonymous with the objective that the Manager must reach a level of excellence and effectiveness which sets him apart from those whom he is managing, he must be an achiever. In this context the Bhagavad Gita enlightens us on all managerial techniques that lead to a harmonious and balanced state overcoming conflict and contradictions which lead to lower efficiency productivity, absence of motivation and lack of work culture.

C) Leadership and Strategy:

Most of the ideas of management concepts like vision, leadership, motivation, excellence in work, goal seeking, work ethics, nature of individual, decision making, external and peripheral levels, planning etc., are already discussed in the Bhagavad Gita and these ideas tackle the issues from the grass roots level of human thinking.

D) Personal and Interpersonal Dynamics and it literature:

Professional always looks for opportunities to encourage employees to engage in their professional development and Research shows that happiness can significantly boost the productivity. Employees who feel motivation from affiliation often have highly developed interpersonal skills that can help them generate strong and meaningful relationships with all internal and external stakeholders.

E) Systems:

Framework of system plays a vital role and the culture of the thinking should reimburse the opportunities lost and thrive towards the encouragement and appreciation of the internal and external stakeholders. Compliments or expressions of gratitude have a bigger impact for the achievement of the intermittent goals.

F) Proactiveness for Innovation within the System:

Measureable goals are a valuable way to stay motivated during the work and a sound tracking system would help you to identify their notable milestones. Celebrating smaller milestone or the long-term milestones and tangible ones can be rewarded. Gratitude and validation are an important part of recognizing those milestones and innovate.

2.2 Management Lessons From Vyasa For Enhancing Effectiveness & Efficiency:

1) Inspiration To Theory of Self-transcendence

2) Prescriptions Of Leadership for Creativity & Innovation

3) Nurturing Great Leaders to Create More Leaders

4) Effective communication

5) Efficient management lies in utilizing resources optimally

1) Inspiration To Theory of Self-transcendence – Answer below questions for basic understanding

- Now let us re-examine some of the modern management concepts in the light of the Bhagavad Gita which is a primer of management by values.
- Question my own field of knowledge
- Commit further to teaching, research & practice

Theory of Self-transcendence propounded in the Gita is overcoming insuperable obstacles in one's path. It involves renouncing egoism, putting others before oneself, team work, dignity, sharing, co-operation, harmony, trust, sacrificing lower needs for higher goals, seeing others in you and yourself in others etc. The portrait of a self-realizing person is that he is a man who aims at his own position and underrates everything else. On the other hand the Self-transcenders are the visionaries and innovators. Their resolute efforts enable them to achieve the apparently impossible Goals and learn to overcome all barriers to reach their goal. In a context that explores the biblical roots of discernment, one may reflect the role and relevance of a study on discernment according to a non-Christian scripture such as the *Bhagavad Gita*. The answer is quite simple. Such an exploration is not only relevant, but also exceptionally helpful and enormously valuable for a deeper understanding of this concept from a fundamentally different perspective. Discernment is after all not merely a Christian concern, but also a perennial human obsession. As Celia Kourie rightly concludes in her article in this volume, an inter-scriptural soul-searching will "contribute to greater insights into the many-faceted splendor of the Ultimate". In our multicultural society, no religion or society can isolate or insulate itself and survive like a living fossil. According to Kourie, tapping into the wisdom of other cultures and religions for mutual understanding and enrichment should be our way forward.

Lesson Learnt from Vysa: The literary style of the *Bhagavad Gita*, demands, necessitates, and provides room for any number of commentaries and interpretations, which becomes an eye-opener and a challenge to those who support and practise scriptural idolatry that takes away the growth potential, plasticity, freedom, and towards the life of their Sacred Scriptures. A generous attitude will keep our windows open to new perspectives and doors to new dives into the ever-deepening realms of divine revelations. Scriptural idolatry can blind people, sapping their energy, turning them into bullies while believing themselves to be defenders of orthodoxy and truth. An occasional glance into analogous concepts found in other religions will, in addition to revealing the complementarities and mutual agreements, save us from forgetting the past that makes people proud, arrogant, and cold towards others. Moreover, as Krishna instructs Arjuna, such comparisons can be regarded as part of our intellectual discernment *cum* scriptural validation (16:24). For example, the *Bhagavad Gita* treats sacrifice - a concept that people often demarcate as a contribution to the milieu of spirituality - from a radically different perspective. Krishna tells Arjuna that acting without attachment is in itself a sacrifice (3:9). He points towards God as the best example for this kind of "perfect action". According to Krishna, God's creative activity was in itself a sacrifice. The world has originated, sustained and is supported through sacrifice. Our vocation as human beings is to collaborate consciously, actively and collectively in this ongoing divine sacrifice.

2) Prescriptions Of Leadership for Creativity & Innovation

In Mahabharata we come across a king called Yayati who, in order to revel in the endless enjoyment of flesh exchanged his old age with the youth of his obliging youngest son for a mythical thousand years. However, he lost himself in the pursuit of sensual enjoyments and felt penitent. He came back to his son pleading to take back his youth. This yayati syndrome shows the externally directed acquisitions, motivations and inner reasoning, emotions and conscience. These syndromes should become the anynomous seeds of creativity and innovation.

The superiority-inferiority complexes emerging from blind egos will not benefit humanity. Any answer given, any discovery made in any corner of the world belongs to the entire human species and to the entire universe. Therefore, turning a blind eye towards, or refusing to open up to the available truths and resources is a crime against oneself, others and God. Such conflict resolution should not be one of the quality of the leadership within an individual.

Let's look at some of the anecdotes from Mahabharata & understand the following:

Leadership Traits , Competencies & Qualities required in the Crisis period:

a) The well informed decision maker :

(More focused & effective contributor & faster accomplishments of goals)

Let us look into the story of Bheema & Jarasandh in Mahabharata. There Bheema kills Jarasandh several times, but miraculously Jarasandh's body recovers each & every time. Then helpless Bheema looks at Shri Krishna. Now, Shri Krishna simply showed Bheema the direction to avoid the joining of the body. He just took a twig, split it into two halves, and then threw it far apart in opposite directions. On seeing this, Bheema did exactly the same with Jarasandh, splitting Jarasandh's body into two halves and throwing it far apart and Jarasandh finally died. Here Shri Krishna could direct Bheema on the right solution to overcome the crisis, only because he was well informed with the correct facts & information. <u>Similarly leaders need to educate themselves quickly, as things are changing very fast in this volatile & uncertain world..</u>

b) **Flexibility / willingness to change &adapt:**

Shri Krishna is said to have several names. One such name that he has been given is '**Ranchod**' which is derived from two different words namely 'Ran' which means war and 'chod' which means to leave. Hence the meaning of **Ranchod** is the one who ran away from the battlefield.

Now, why did he evade the war? Simple; It was a clear strategy from Krishna. He wanted to avoid the destruction, the loss of people's lives, and wealth & economy that arises as a consequence of the war. Shri Krishna was flexible to shift his capital from Mathura to Dwarka, simply to avoid the war with Jarasandh and thus showed us the importance of having flexibility in everything that we do by demonstrating the opulence of renunciation which is the quality of the eminent personality of a leader.

c) <u>Motivational skills: (Leader as a motivator):</u>

In the story of Mahabharata, At the Battlefield of Kurukshetra, Arjuna lost his motivation to fight & was paralyzed to inaction. Shri Krishna motivated him to act, irrespective of the results of his actions. **As Bhagavad Gita says, "Not to worry or desire for the result but perform one's karma"** and thus steered Arjuna to action.

Similarly the great leaders must be able to show the clear picture to others and should be free from all self doubts from one's mind. In short, leaders uphold Dharma (**what is right** in any situation)& also motivate the follower to perform Nishkama Karma (**selfless**

actions).Compassion at a time of crisis is a very important manifestation of leadership which is deteriorating in recent trend.

This theory is practiced by Smt.Indra Nooyi, formor chairman of Pesico co.Pvt.Ltd., USA; by giving space and opportunity to the younger people in the team and she gave freedom for the execution of their ideas if they were innovative.

d) Leaders are always Goal Oriented:

Shri Krishna's life goals were very clear & simple.

1. **ParitranayaSadhunam**: Deliver the pious; Welfare for Good.

2. **Vinashaya Cha dushkritam**: Annihilate the miscreants (Destroy the evil)

3. **Dharma – Samastha - Panarthaya:** (reestablish the good principles)

The Goals of life was very clear to Shri Krishna, that's why he could completely focus on it &he finally achieved it. To be successful in any situation, goals has to be set and invest dedicated efforts to achieve. The entire story of Mahabharata is based on several crisis & it's effective management strategy of disciple, focus, and self-less dedication. Pandavas & Kauravas had soldiers in an uneven ratio (7: 11). It clearly reflects that the entire battle (crisis) was won with effective strategies.

In today's crisis situation, there's no ready-made play book available for leaders showing particular strategy for peculiar event. In this situation when we look into Hindu Mythology, where Shri Krishna is considered to be one of the biggest leaders of all times, We can learn the personal traits to be imbibed, competencies to be inculcated, and qualities & behaviours to be inbuilt within oneself to display the real character of an individual.

A quick list of following is helpful for building a good charismatic of a leader. The entire Bhagavad Gita is the sharing of learning --

1. Friendly approach to all
2. Accessible to all
3. Listening to our inner voice (instinct)

4. Perseverance
5. Long term goals
6. Sharing the Learning
7. Transparent Communication for open & Timely way
8. Grit & Determination
9. Curiosity
10. Self-Control
11. Positivism/Optimism
12. Sense of Gratitude
13. Resilience
14. Social intelligence
15. Agility & Adaptability
16. Compassion
17. Calmness & Confidence
18. Motivating, Coaching, Counselling

3) Nurturing Great Leaders To Create More Leaders

If there was anyone in the Ramayana who was having best of the managerial characteristics then it was Sughriv. He showed traits of a great manager by getting Ram to work consequently and getting back his kingdom from brother stronger than him. His managerial skills are seen in other instances as well, especially when he had Angad to work for him. Imagine Sughriv to be a mediocre manager; Angad could become one of their arch-rivals.

A good leader proves time and again that businesses run on a good relationship. And an ideal manager would value good relations with the employees, clients etc, to make it count for the organization. Lord Ram was one such master of fostering good relations.

When Hanuman successfully discovered Sita's whereabouts, he, on his own choice, set aflame the city of Lanka. This decision of

Hanuman disgruntled Ram. This led to Hanuman not taking further decisions for his own.

Consider this scenario in the war where Mahiravan abducted Ram and Lakshman with intent to drag them to the Patal Lok. It was Hanuman who had the right intellect and physical prowess to rescue them. Eventually, Hanuman succeeded in rescuing Ram and Lakshman. What Ram did here is something that every leader should be learning – creating more leaders within the organization to succeed in achieving a common goal. A true leader is the one who creates leaders around. This is a very steep task but when followed with caution, it will have people around within the organization who are capable of taking independent decisions for collective good. Essentially, a good leader will always choose to groom potential managers and employees to ensure long-term retention.

Lessons mentioned in the Vyasa: According to the *Gita,* there are three *margas* (ways) available to us to attain freedom, namely *karma* (action), *bhakthi* (devotion) and *jnana* (knowledge). They are not watertight compartments. They are merely three stages of the one and the same path, the goal being transcendence from the servitude of the known and the unknown. Transcendence is a human potential, even though all have *nama-rupa* (name and form); only those who attempt to realise this potential can be considered truly human in its proper sense. Bhagwad Gita disseminates the need of discerning capacity of an humans to be free from proudness and the arrogance.

4) Effective communication

When something important is communicated, stick to it! We all know about the battle of Bali and demon Mayavee. One of their fights landed in the cave wherein Sugreeva was ordered by Bali to stay out and keep a watch over the cave till the time he emerges back.It was almost a year' wait. And neither of Bali or the Mayavee (demon) came out. Sugreeva 'thought' they must have killed each other in the battle. And therefore, he returned to Kishkindha (their kingdom) and took the ruler's throne while also marrying Tara, Bali's wife to be his.Nevertheless, Bali returned later seeing Sugreeva as king and his wife as Sugreeva's wife, Bali felt betrayed.

Lessons mentioned in the Vyasa:

The root cause of fatal enmity between the two brothers – Sugreeva and Bali had its root in awful miscommunication. A managerial lesson here is to beware of miscommunication at any point within the organization – be it acquisition or in talent management. Above all one should have faith on another's word and verifying about the situation before leaping to final decision.

3) Efficient management lies in utilizing resources optimally:

Ram represents a skillful manager, utilizing the available resources optimally to gain maximum out of minimum. These skills are evident even during the war with Ravana. The crucial one was the act of building a bridge over the sea to reach Lanka. While there were a lot of thoughts on how to cross the Sea, Ram took 3 days for meditating and later on suggested to create a bridge. He picked up the right people for that job; two of his army men – Nal and Nila. They were skilled in making a bridge and constructing things. Ram also gathered local tribals (the apemen), got them trained from his team to help Nal and Nila build the bridge at earliest. The bridge was constructed within a few days and thereafter, helped Ram and his army to reach Lanka.

Lessons mentioned in the Vyasa:

Pick up the right people for the right task according to their talent and skill. A good management scenario is to have all the people giving their best. People should be motivated as per their requisition of needs.

Ramayana is one of such Indian Epics that has a vast potential to change our every-day human life. Be it in the management or in personal life, it never ceases to inspire us in small instances even after ages.

Drawing conclusions from this Epic Mythology

- Form and lay a strategic vision and mission that serves the value system.
- A good leader is the one who orchestrates the entire conduction of an event that delivers expected results

- Break your big plans in small pieces based on periodic strategies and annual plan with reference to the target.
- Always evaluate your triumphs based on the available resources and its ownership to the immediate strategy.

2.3 Management Lessons of Bhagavad Gita for Individuals For Managerial Effectiveness

a) Receive with an open mind

One of the popular verses of the Gita advises "detachment" from the fruits or results of actions performed in the course of one's duty. Being dedicated towards work has to mean "working with passion for generating excellence for its own sake." One of the main reasons for non-attachment to results is because workings of the world are not designed to positively respond to our calculations and hence expected fruits may not always be forthcoming. While the Gita also advises the avarice of selfish gains by discharging one's accepted duty, and further does not absolve anybody of the consequences arising from discharge of his responsibilities.

b) Assimilate and levitate the Opportunities

Basically to assimilate the data to be collected should be according to the needs of your affiliation and its path of growth. Affiliation demand consistency and loyalty for longer duration. Though one may have connected with the short term goal presently but focus should be for long-term goals. Mastery in any profession can happen with visionary and consistency. Assembling unwanted data indulges waste of time and this time should be utilized properly at optimum. Time management in this process too matters because when measure the time of handling the error in monetary terms initialization with the identification, searching, rectification, etc., than we are incurring huge intangible loss. For this purpose we need to be very careful.

For achievement there needs to be a growth. Changes depend on your choices. Few factors to mention that influences are the nourishments required for growth + purpose to be live + people/environment to sustain the goal. Change yourself and your environment, growth will be faster and more successful. A better growth environment won't help you much if you don't do everything in your power to make the most of it. You must seize the growth opportunities you have and make the most of them by challenging yourself and never ever dwell on your past.

c) Reinforce The Compliments:

One of the most defining moments of Ramayana is the moment when Ram's father King Dasharatha, in order to fulfill his promise to one of his queen Kaikeyi, crowns her son Bharata as the king of Ayodhya and sends Ram to the forest instead for fourteen years. This happens at a time when the whole kingdom was preparing for Ram to be crowned their new king. Many times at the workplace, the same situation plays out-a hardworking employee who should be rewarded and promoted for his work, is sidetracked and instead, the boss promotes his or her favourite. This can lead to discontent among employees and make them feel that they are working at an unfair workplace, leading to a loss in engagement, productivity and ultimately leading to attrition. While in Ramayana, Dasharatha was bound by his word that he had given to Kaikeyi earlier, bosses of today should not be limited by any such biases in order to ensure a fair workplace where everyone is inspired to give his best. Nevertless, don't ever support the promises which breaks the strong bonding adherent in the organization.

d) Voluntarily Rung the Character Ladder for the Organization:

During the fight between Ram and Ravan's army, Lakshman was so badly wounded in the battle it seemed that he would die before sunrise. The monkeys and bears decided that Hanuman must leap to the Himalayas and bring back the healing herb from the Medicine Mountain to save Lakshman's life. So Hanuman leapt over the ocean and travelled across India to the Himalayas. Once there, it took him a long time to find the fabled Medicine Mountain. Hanuman found it at last -covered with herbs, but he didn't know which one of them was the magic healing herb. So he wrapped his arms around the whole mountain, pulled it out of the ground and lifted it onto the palms of his hand. He then flew with the mountain back to Lanka.

This incident reminds us of a crucial aspect in the modern workforce: Employees going the extra mile in ways that contribute to their organization and their peer's success. The behavior portrayed by Hanuman mirrors the role of your engaged employee who is willing to go beyond their formal roles by helping out coworkers, volunteering to take on special assignments, introducing new ideas and work practices, attending non-mandatory meetings, putting in extra hours to complete important projects, and so forth. One should extend cordial support to them and be aloof from egoism and jealousy.

e) Embrace Creativity & Innovation

Individuals should be very competitive to maintain a high standard in their profession and work ethic. Awards for the excellent performance would motivate the persons to strongly desire for recognition. Below are few strategies to inculcate qualities of skill:

1. Raise new questions and good questions are the heart of reflection of one's character.
2. Build new answers
3. Move beyond your Limiting Beliefs
4. Add value with potentiality for self-esteem
5. Enriching thinking after intentional pausing
6. Incubation of listening and learning
7. Always Positivity in life

f) Grace Eternal tangible and Intangible strengths:

Some persons are interested in influencing others and making an impression in the workplace and these persons are influenced by the theory of leadership where they take initiatives to resolve the issues in the organization and acknowledge that all the work is done through their sagacity as they have ability to govern and disciple ones by the use of reason. Such persons have the leadership skills alongwith good judgements while taking final decisions.

In Ramayan, Lakshman draws the protective line famously known as 'Lakshmanrekha', to protect Sita, his sister in law from the demons in the forest that could harm her. However, when the Rakshasa king Ravan comes disguised as mendicant, Sita unsuspectingly crosses the protective line and gets into trouble as Ravan abducts her.'Lakshmanrekha' in the context of the workplace and business symbolizes the security layer, which is important for the safety of intellectual capital. The ongoing trend of data breaches and the increasing privacy risks associated with social media continues to be a national and international concern. The world of work is becoming more and more digital and the data privacy is under threat. As organizations across the globe invest heavily in information technology (IT) to deploy the best of cyber defense capabilities, employees have to also comply with these rules and regulations for their company's and their consumer's benefit. With data breaches and cyber-attacks anticipated to increase in the due course of time, it is critical that employees become more aware about the 'Lakshmanrekha' (data security), understand its importance and follow the protocols. When it comes to data protection, one must not cross the 'Lakshmanrekha'.

It is the common experience that the spirit of grievances from the clerk to the Director is identical and only their scales and composition vary. It should have been that once the lower-order needs are more than satisfied, the Director should have no problem in optimizing his contribution to the organization. But more often than not, it does not happen like that; the eagle soars high but keeps its eyes firmly fixed on the dead animal below. The work must be done with detachment of jealously, egoism, envy, etc., which spoils the work.

The disinterested work finds expression in devotion, surrender and equipoise. The former two are psychological while the third is the strong-willed determination to keep the mind free of and above the dualistic pulls of daily experiences. Detached involvement in work is the key to mental equanimity or the state of **Nirdwanda**. This attitude leads to a stage where the worker begins to feel the presence of the Supreme Intelligence guiding the empirical individual intelligence. Such de-personified intelligence is best suited for those who sincerely believe in the supremacy of organizational goals as compared to narrow personal success and achievement. The principle of reducing our attachment to personal gains from the work done or controlling the aversion to personal losses enunciated in Ch.2 Verse 47(as mentioned below) of the Gita is the foolproof prescription for attaining equanimity. The common apprehension about this principle that it will lead to lack of incentive for effort and work, striking at the very root of work ethic, is not valid because the advice is to be judged as relevant to man's overriding quest for true mental happiness. Thus while the common place theories on motivation lead us to bondage, the Gita theory takes us to freedom and real happiness of performing work with obligatory and transcendental knowledge.

g) One Should be Nyayatik-

Three stone-cutters were engaged in erecting a temple. As usual, a H.R.D. Consultant asked them what they were doing. The response of the three workers to this innocent-looking question is illuminating. 'I am a poor man. I have to maintain my family. I am making a living here,' said the first stone-cutter with a dejected face. Well, I work because I want to show that I am the best stone-cutter in the country,' said the second one with a sense of pride. 'Oh, I want to build the most beautiful temple in the country,' said the third one with a visionary gleam. Their jobs were identical but their perspectives were different. Bhagwad Gita has already specified to us to develop the visionary perspective in the work we do and exaggerate the passion for the work. For this purpose, we need personality traits as under:

- GUNAS- Vedas do mention the three gunas namely Sattva (goodness), Rajas (passion, desires) and Tamas (darkness, relative unawareness, lethargy). One should always have Satavik guna where you have righteous mind though one is involved in the business because Tamas are better known as Mansa dosha. One should be Virtuous who illustrates their behavior with highest moral standards. Mention of 3 trigunas namely Satwa, Rajas and Tamas are the three essential energies of the mind. The pscycological characteristics of an individual are genetically dependent on the relative dominance of the three gunas. Alongwith gunas one needs to have the attitude of Tyga. Ignorance about the silly things done by stupid peoples because Jgyani people always think before they act to avoid to look to as an idiot. Wrong Knowledge is the discrepancies enacted by the less intellectual people and the intellectual people never ever doubt about their act which are the symbol of high standards.

Management Lessons For Life Skills:

Ch.2 Verse 47- from Bhagwad Gita:
Lord Krishna –

>   **Karmanyevadhikaraste**
>   **MaphaleshuKadachan**
>   **Makarmaphelheturbho**
>   **Mate Sansostawakarmam**

You have a right to perform your prescribed duties, but you are not entitled to the fruits of your actions. Never consider yourself to be the cause of the results of your activities, nor be attached to inaction.

3.1 Strategies To Grow & Lead:
1)   Time to be Growth Conscious
It is time to stop being goal conscious which defines your destination, motivates other too to support you and challenges you to work consistently but it is seasonal till your goals are reached. Growth consciousness focuses on the journey which is lifelong and it matures other too alongwith you. It changes you and keeps you growing beyond the goal. Alignment of methods of motivation with your personality type is very important. It's difficult to remain engaged in anything if you have not found a way to value and appreciate the process. Make a list of everything you like about personal growth and if your list is very short than really you have to work on it.

2)   Attributes of Learning by embracing strategy with honesty & commitment
➢   Systematic Approach for becoming highly strategic
•   Wisdom of Knowledge through Investigation, Incubation, Illumination, Illustration

Seeking knowledge can be through learning and another by experience. But Evaluated experience is the best teacher. One have to try your intention with solidarity to expand the three I's as mentioned above. Everyone think life is pretty straightforward and simple theory of longer live, learning, experience and acquire more knowledge but life has a way of becoming complicated. Designing life is more important than designing your career because when one plans for life then career will work itself out. There is no warm-up for life, no dress rehearsal, yet people regret over not being proactive enough. To develop strategies, depend on systems. More accomplishments in life comes more easily if you approach them strategically. Rarely does a haphazard approach to anything succeed. Systems leverage your time, money and abilities. One has to cultivate curiosity to go out and acquire knowledge, understanding and wisdom. Learn something new every day. First, you must wake up by seeing the everyday as having opportunities to learn by incubating it. Incubation is listening and learning. Illumination is the discovery where the proverbial lightbulb turns on. Comprehension by Illustration is most effective by good ideas which are like study of skeleton.

Below are Yogas in Bhagwad-Gita:

Karma yoga: Karma Yoga or Karma which means action. According to the holy scripture, one should perform his/her duty or actions without thinking of the outcome. One should act selflessly without any expectations from the outcome.

Bhakti yoga: It is considered one of the easiest forms of yoga. This form of yoga lays emphasis on the power of devotion and love between God and his disciple. It advises an individual to get absorbed in the supreme soul, that is, God.

Jnana yoga: This yoga suggests that people should seek 'Jnana' or knowledge to enlighten their lives. Bhagavad Gita advocates that by attaining knowledge, one can attain salvation.

Karma Vairagya yoga: As per Bhagavad Gita Karma Vairagya yoga teaches humans to choose the path of action and sacrifice. The Holy Scriptures considers Karma and renunciation as means to liberation.

Paramhamsa Vijnana or Vigyana yoga: The Paramhamsa Vijnana enlightens a person to take the path of realizing the ultimate truth.

Dhyana or Abhyasa yoga: This is the sixth chapter of Bhagavad Geeta teaches an individual about the importance of meditation. It suggests that people who perform Dhyana yoga are able to concentrate deeper.

Visadh yoga: Whenever dilemmas cloud over mind, an individual performs Visadh yoga.

Sankhya yoga: As per the holy scripture, Sankhya yoga is popularly known as the yoga of analysis. This form of yoga is about logical reasoning and intellect.

Raja Vidya yoga: It teaches an individual to please Para Brahman to gain secret knowledge. Raja Vidya yoga is also known as yoga through the king of sciences.

Vibhuti Vistara yoga: This guides people to focus on the path of godliness. Vibhuti Vistara yoga is performed through appreciating the infinite opulence of God.

Vishwaroopa Darshana yoga: The Bhagavad Gita advocates that one can obtain the omnipresent form of the supreme being. Vishwaroopa Darshana yoga also means yoga through beholding the cosmic form of God.

Kshetra Kshetrejna Vibhaga yoga: Through this form of yoga, the Gita advises an individual to give up ego. This yoga is about associating the supreme being with nature, man, and intellect.

Gunatraya Vibhaga yoga: Gunatraya Vibhaga yoga or yoga through understanding the three modes of material nature. It requires people to understand three qualities, which are Sattvic, Rajasic and Tamasic.

Purushottama yoga: It is also known as the yoga of supreme divine personality wherein an individual learns about the infinite nature of the supreme being.

Daivasura Sampad Vibhaga yoga: As per Bhagavad Gita, one should learn the difference between evil and divine qualities, therefore Daivasura Sampad Vibhaga yoga helps in it.

Aksara Parabrahman yoga: This form of yoga in the holy Gita talks about the immortal nature of the Para Brahman.

Shraddhatraya Vibhaga yoga: It teaches a person the understanding of goodness, passion and ignorance in life. Basically, a person should be aware of his actions and thoughts.

Moksha Upadesha yoga: The last and 18th form of yoga in Gita is the Moksha Upadesha yoga. It teaches a person to detach from worldly distractions and surrender to God.

Assimilation of the ideas of different yogas of the Gita leads us to the wider spectrum of lokasamgraha or general welfare which is Jnanyoga. There is also another dimension in the work ethic. If the karmayoga is blended with bhaktiyoga then the work itself becomes worship, a seva yoga. Performance of our duty with selfless motive and principles is essential. So Bhagavad Gita discusses in great details the theory of cause and effect, making the doer responsible for the consequences of his deeds. Stress management principles are described in details in several verses acting as a brilliant guide to the operating Manager for psychological energy conservation and avoidance of burn-outs in the work situations. Thus the best means for effective work performance is to become the work itself. Attaining this state of nishkama karma is the right attitude to work because it prevents the ego, the mind from dissipation through speculation on future gains or losses. It has been presumed for long that satisfying lower needs of a worker like adequate food, clothing and shelter, recognition, appreciation, status, personality development etc are the key factors in the motivational theory of personnel management.

- There is no point in weeping over the inevitable

Courage and character teaches to care but ineffective character teaches to be callous. One has to possess good character to be committed towards the principles and moral values of life. Another way to retain is zero-tolerance or ignore the arrogant who don't follow these principles. Fulfilling the promises mad is also one kind of commitment and these are intensely practiced during ancient vyasa period. The battle in Ramayana was fought to set an example in front of society to follow the value system created by society. Under the name of selfish interest, there must be a zero-tolerance policy for the culprits. Ravan was a culprit who abducted Sita and wanted to marry her forcefully. Therefore, **Ram killed Ravan**. Every company has some value system. All the employees must understand its significance and learn to follow to avoid strict and penal action against them. The entire Ramayan is an epitome of ethics. **Ravan tricked Sita** and **kidnapped** her in the absence of Ram. Even then Ram always followed ethical steps to take Sita back. He sent Hanuman with a warning to leave Sita or get into a battle ethically. He kept giving warnings to Ravan to follow the right path before he finally killed him. Secondly, committed towards promise made which was executed by Lord Rama and Arjuna. Queen Kaikayi, the real mother of Bharata, demanded Ram to go to the forest in exile for **14 years** and Bharat to take over as the king. King Dashrath was shattered but when Ram came to know he obliged to his father's commitments. It teaches us fulfilling commitment under whatever circumstances. Ram followed his father's commitment. It should be understood by all the managers, executives and employees in a company. Everyone in a company must put effort into fulfilling the commitment given by the manager or representative to the entities or individuals of the external environment.

3) **Stretching for Change of Significance**

Most people use only a small fraction of their ability to strive for achieving the perfection. Tailor-made setting and edging is required for full usage of your potentials with consistent dedication but many people are willing to settle for the average of their life. To achieve perfection one has to work beyond their comfort zones which leads to mediocrity. We are responsible for our own outcome and we defend ourselves by covering it up with the reasons. We need to change it, grow from it and forge a new path. Stretching should start from oneself. Innovation and progress are often initiated by the person who wants to push change. To bring change one needs to take risk to learn faster and they learn how to solve problems with optimum utility of resources.

When Sita was abducted by Ravan, the king of Lanka; Lord Ram showed spectacular skills of leading an army of monkeys. His first prominent quality as a leader was of being a visionary. His vision was to **rescue Sita from Ravan** and overcome all the difficulties in between. His second prominent quality was to be an effective motivator to the army. His army developed a special skills to face the enemy by coming out of their comfort zone. They observed that stones/pebbles should be of particular dimensions and the name of Lord Rama helped it to float on the surface of the water. This is an art and a study of science involved which is the definition of management.

Ram was also responsible for delegating the right responsibility to the right person. Hanuman was given the responsibility to find out where Sita was in Lanka. The engineers **Nal and Neel** were given the task to design the bridge from India to Sri Lanka. It was an engineering marvel that today has the potential to generate electricity for millions of years because of radioactive material in it.

4) Make Smart Trade-offs

Learn to see trade-offs as opportunities for growth. Identify the pulses and minuses that are the hard cores of facts which can lead you to discover the tendency to overestimate/underestimate of the real value. Change is required for the smart trade-offs. Most trade-offs can be made at any time. The higher the clib, tougher the trade-offs. The list of trade-off principles start by using spark ideas:

1. Am willing to give up financial security today for potential tomorrow

2. Am willing to give up immediate gratification for only personal growth or building a character

3. Am willing to give up the fast life for the good life

4. Am willing to give up addition for multiplication

The important things in life usually take longer than we expect and cost more than we anticipate. So you have to just multiply by 2 to compensate. If you think a project will take a week to accomplish, allot two. Of you think a goal will require Rupees one thousand then set aside Rupees 2000. It is found that multiplying everything with two infuses realism into optimism.

The construction of Ram Setu, the bridge, did not take place with any heavy and advanced technological equipment. It was the result of brilliant coordination directed and performed by Nal and Neel. The entire army of monkey soldiers set a great example of coordination for making the first-ever bridge of the world. Building the bridge (Ram Setu) from India to Sri Lanka was not an easy task. It needed manpower and teamwork which was contributed by all the monkey soldiers and their leaders including Sugriv, Jamvant, Hanuman, Nal, and Neel. It is considered as the first-ever made bridge of the world in the history of mankind.

5) Always prepare for the worst Consequences of the action –

There was a day when Ravan's son Meghnad killed Laxman during the battle. Ram delegated the responsibility of bringing **Sanjeevani** (the medicine to save Laxman's life). Hanuman outperformed and brought the entire mountain called Dronagiri or Gandhmardan from the Himalayas. Hanuman exhibited excellent skills of decision-making by deciding to take the mountain if he was not able to identify the medicine. Lord Hanuman was an unbeatable superhero! Such decision-making skills must be developed in not only the managers but also the executives in times of need.

Similarly, always prepare well in advance and be ready to face the worst too in case it incurs. Ram and Bharat were half-brothers but they loved each other. Ram was more attached to Bharat than Shatrughan who was his real brother. The height of Bharat's dedication crossed its limit when he made Ram promise to return as soon as the tenure of 14 years would be over otherwise he would commit suicide. Ram could return with Sita only after killing Ravan. He set a wonderful example of **managing the worst situation by planning** all the events very well and managed to reach on time before Bharat. Every employee must learn the importance of timely production and delivery of the products and services to the customers to avoid the risk of losing them.

6) Well-Defined problem – is half solved

When Ram got to know that Sita was in Lanka, he set his mission to reach there and rescue her come what may! He was a king but during exile, he did not go back to his kingdom to take an army. He managed to arrange an army, reach Lanka and won the battle to fulfill his mission. He faced many difficulties but he managed to get the work done not only by human beings but also animals. Getting the work done is the simplest definition of management. Ram was one of the greatest managers in India. He accomplished his mission by showing commendable managerial skills. His determination is worth learning by all the employees as every company has a mission statement. Everyone in the company should take it as if it is his own and work towards it.

Attitude should be as per the norms of YOGA mentioned below. Yoga is the means of setting attitude towards learning, attaining the path for the performance and driving with perfection for excellence which is the ultimate aim of life. Alway's have a beginner's mind-set. Ask why? Explore by spending time with other curious people. Curious people ask questions. Good questions are the heart of reflection. Because there is something about a well-worded question that often penetrates to the heart of the matter and triggers new ideas and insights. Ramayan is an epic that is used in the present times to teach various lessons on management and morality.

Resource Based view of individuals and organizations for Success of a business and industrial enterprise depends to a large extent on the proper utilization of resources. A good organization must be capable of overcoming the problems of an enterprise and capable in achieving the predetermined objects of enterprise. For this, adherence of measuring the tangibles and intangibles' and its achievable is equally important. A good organization should divide the functions of an enterprise in such a manner so that plans may be implemented easily and successfully. A very important essential element of co-ordination in a good organization is that there must be harmonious adjustment across various functions and foremost further, there must not be the repetition of activities. Co-ordination is the essence of management. Therefore, all the activities of an organization must be prudently co-ordinated. Span of authority with adequate number of subordinates facilitates high possibility of effective control and achieving the targets. Adequate flexibility according to the requisites of changing circumstances is to be framed in such a manner that all the employees may contribute their efforts in their execution. Therefore, all the functions of the organization must be of the nature that they may be executed easily and economically.

3.2 Different Strategies To Learn:

1) Driving with Motive rather than only objective of Context

The driving forces in today's rat-race are speed and greed as well as ambition and competition. The natural fallout from these forces is erosion of one's ethico-moral fibre which supersedes the value system as a means in the entrepreneurial path like tax evasion, undercutting, spreading canards against the competitors, entrepreneurial spying, instigating industrial strife in the business rivals' establishments etc. Although these practices are taken as normal business hazards for achieving progress, they always end up as a pursuit of mirage -the more the needs the more the disappointments. This phenomenon may be called as yayati-syndrome. Here we conclude that one needs to concentrate on logical reasoning for taking ethical decision. Motive should be the influential factor and the objective should be mere purpose for achieving the goal. Below are the ways to analyse things:

- Gap between
- Similarities and differences
- Patterns and peculiarities
- Independence and interdependence
- Continuities and discontinuities
- Evolution and Eureka

2) Simulations for Endowments with Resource–

The first lesson in the management science is to choose wisely and utilize optimally the scarce resources if one has to succeed in his venture. During the curtain raiser before the Mahabharata War Duryodhana chose Sri Krishna's large army for his help while Arjuna selected Sri Krishna's wisdom for his support. This episode gives us a clue as to who is an Effective Manager. Over the centuries numerous attempts have been made to figure out and attribute symbolic meanings to the events and personalities in the *Bhagavad-Gita*. Leaving aside the complex issue of assigning symbolic meanings to every person named in the battle narrative, it is not difficult to figure out the basic symbolism. This world in which we live is a *dharmakshetra,* a field upon which we act out our *svadharma* (vocation/ duty/inherent obligation) according to our character or our innate constitution. The quality of our emotions, mind, intellect, and will depends on our present level of evolution. It is not merely in the world, but even within ourselves that we find all kinds of negative impulses, conflicts, confusions, fears, and ignorance. Although, at times, deep within ourselves, we could sense an attraction towards divinity, it is often overruled by a multitude of impulses to delusion. However, it is to be noted that all the warriors of ignorance and delusion are children of a blind ego (Dhritarashtra), whereas the inner soldiers of truth and higher consciousness are the children of the Spirit-Self, the divine *Atman*. Kurukshetra is the personality. *Buddhi* (mind/intellect) of the individual is the charioteer who tries to lead the true self to attain enlightenment. This aspiration for truth evokes opposition from within one's own mind and body, governed by the blind ego. Thus begins the war between Pandavas and Kauravas, good and evil, truth and falsehood, ignorance and wisdom, trying to annihilate each other. The most surprising feature of this inner war is that many insightful and honest "virtues" are lining up in support of the "worthless". For example, the ego, which is the creation of ignorance and delusion, torments the individual self as a result of his/her fears, desires and illusions. It manages to line up the *bona fide* human qualities to defend and ensure its survival under the pretext that the individual's survival is intertwined with his/her own survival. Individuals who use their intellectual faculties to achieve the goals dictated by their blind instincts are yet another example of this phenomenon. As a result, along with the Kauravas, most of the "Pandava" army is also eliminated in the eventual transformation of the individual into a higher state of being.

3) Learning by Rules of Competitions

SWOT (Strength, Weakness, Opportunities and Threats) assessments behind the decisions with assumptions. Actions after completeness of thinking through & thinking across the problem for the accurate solution are feasible to achieve. Decisions should be to overcome the obstacles of present situation after evaluating the past performance towards the realistic and innovative future with the expected change. Weakness has to be converted into strength. E.g. While searching for Sita who was eloped to unknown place, Lord Rama converted this weakness by seeking help of versatile person like Sugriv and Hanuman. Meticulous planning with perservance of patience and skill is equally important. Everyday action with smile is crucial to succeed in future. Practise what you preach and following rules to be at it. Monitoring these actions at timely interval and improvising it if required is the rule of the demand.

4) Learning from a Mentor possessing premium KASH

Learning from a Mentor those who have superior KASH (Knowledge, Attitude, Skillful, Habit) or enriched with qualities that are different from you. In Hindu Mythology, Shri Krishna is considered as "The greatest Crisis manager". His name is synonymous with great intelligence, effective communication, Pure Compassion, Love affection. The remarkable ability is to solve any crisis at any time faced by his followers. In today's challenging times, we are also looking for such type of leaders as Shri Krishna, who can manage the present crisis & offer some silver bullets to the world by his knowledge and skill. Apparently humble humane attitude is his character. Habits which are practiced everyday with full determination and commitments transforms into a character. Henceforth, one has the choice to select good or bad habits which becomes the personality traits of an individual. We can conclude that just a thought can influence the building process of the character. So, good character mentor is very essential in life.

5) Learn by observations

A visionary individual engages all their senses to see the unshown, hear the unspoken and feel the articulated events well in anticipation.

Consequences of a action should be analysed and measured in terms of its magnitude of impact upon one's karma and dharma. E.g.

Finance Lessons from the Holy Gita || CH 3, 35 || śhreyānswa-dharmoviguṇahpara-dharmātsv-anuṣhṭhitātswa-dharmenidhanaṁshreyahpara-dharmobhayāvahaḥ "It is far better to perform one's duties perfectly than to imitate someone's duties. Destruction in the course of performing one's own duty is better than engaging in another's duties, to follow another's path is dangerous".

6) Learn by Experimentation

Do something different from what you have been doing before. When the Vanara Army reached the seashore, they were not unable to figure out a way to cross the sea. Lord Ram motivated his army to have self-belief that they will turn the impossible into possible. Lord Ram told them about the importance of teamwork, and the entire army worked in a planned manner and found a solution to the problem. The significance of teamwork still remains as critical as it was then. An organization that functions as a team has the most chance of surviving in any given condition. And team work brings the best of minds, thoughts, ideas, and the workforce for any project.

7) Learn with optimal approach

Before a start, always answer below questions:
➢ What went right and not wrong?
➢ What was deviation and what was not?
➢ Why & why?

The answer for these questions should not be only for maximization but for optimal outcomes. Work culture means vigorous and arduous effort in pursuit of a given or chosen task. When Bhagawan Sri Krishna rebukes Arjuna in the strongest words for his unmanliness and imbecility in recoiling from his righteous duty it is nothing but a clarion call for the highest work culture. Poor work culture is the result of tamoguna overtaking one's mindset. Bhagawan's stinging rebuke is to bring out the temporarily dormant rajoguna in Arjuna. In Chapter 16 of the Gita Sri Krishna elaborates on two types of Work Ethic viz. daivi sampat or divine work culture and asuri sampat or demonic work culture.

Daivi work *culture* - means fearlessness, purity, self-control, sacrifice, straightforwardness, self-denial, calmness, absence of fault-finding, absence of greed, gentleness, modesty, absence of envy and pride.

Asuri work *culture* - means egoism, delusion, desire-centric, improper performance, work which is not oriented towards service.

It is to be noted that mere action is not enoughas much as a hardened criminal has also a very good work culture. Action should be conditioned by reality and ethics. The Gardner may water the plants everday or water the plants with a hundred buckets, but the fruit arrives only if it is fully grown or is in it's season. Critical analysis is the must for such study of optimization.

8) Learn by wearing shoes of a character

Gita tells us not to mortgage the present commitment to an uncertain future. If we are not able to measure up to this height, then surly the fault lies with us and not with the teaching. Some people argue that being unattached to the consequences of one's action would make one un-accountable as accountability is a much touted word these days with the vigilance department sitting on our shoulders. However, we have to understand that the entire second chapter has arisen as a sequel to the temporarily lost sense of accountability on the part of Arjuna in the first chapter of the Gita in performing his swadharma.

9) Thriving For Mastery, Not Slaves Of Nature

Krishna instructs Arjuna about the inherent *gunas* (qualities) of *prakrti* (nature/matter). Being material, we have inherited those qualities. Yet, we are not destined to be governed by those natural qualities (3:28). However, having transcended the control of nature does not give anyone the right to scorn the ignorant, who are still under its yoke. The liberated should be compassionate towards them and should be willing to help them. Those who are completely deluded by the *gunas* of *prakrti* remain attached to those *gunas* and actions; the man of perfect knowledge should not unsettle the mind of those insufficiently knowing fools. (3:30).

Secondly, It is the forgetfulness of the past that makes people proud. Presenting himself as an example; Krishna clarifies the difference between an enlightened person and an ordinary person: says "Arjuna, you and I have passed through many births. I remember them all; you do not remember." (4:5). It is the forgetfulness of the past that makes people proud, arrogant, and cold towards others. Krishna then reveals another fact about action to Arjuna: says "He, who sees inaction in action, and action in inaction, is wise among men; he is a yogi, who has performed all actions." (4:18). Running away from action or finding false justification for our failures to act will not make us wise or masters of our nature. On the earth there is no purifier as great as Knowledge; he who has attained purity of heart through a prolonged practice of *karma yoga* (action without attachment) automatically sees the light of Truth in the self in course of time, assures Krishna (4:38).

Whose Lesson Is The Best? Arjuna Or Hanuman Or Ravanna

4.1.1 Lessons for Arjun from Krishna –
1) PROFESSION IS RIGHTEOUS DUTY

We do not know which is preferable for us - to fight or not to fight; nor do we know whether we shall win or whether they will conquer us. Those very sons of Dhrtharashtra, killing whom, we do not even wish to live, stand in the enemy ranks. (2:6).By way of clearing the confusion of Arjuna, Lord Krishna first tries to shed some light on the mental state of Arjuna who was arguing with Krishna like a learned person. However, Krishna points out that his sorrow and grief indicate that he is not yet wise, because "wise men do not sorrow over the living or the dead" (2:11). Krishna again clarifies that, for a wise man, pain and pleasure are alike (2:15). This is because the unreal has no existence, and the real never ceases to be; the reality of both has thus been perceived by the seers of the truth (2:16). Krishna clarifies to Arjuna that the soul is eternal, omnipresent, immovable, constant and everlasting (2:24); so there is no need for him to mourn for this transitory body which is designed to perish sooner or later. Krishna reminds Arjuna of the duty that is assigned to him as a soldier: "... there is nothing more welcome for a man of the warrior class than a righteous war" (2:31). Krishna continues: "Now, if you refuse to fight this righteous war, then, shrinking your duty and losing your reputation, you will incur sin" (2:33). According to Krishna, Arjuna, being a warrior by profession, should be ready to accept both life and death. Die, and you will win heaven; conquer, and you will enjoy sovereignty of the earth; therefore, stand up, Arjuna, determined to fight. Treating alike victory and defeat, gain and loss, pleasure and pain, get ready for the fight, then; fighting thus you will not incur sin (2:37-38).

2) ATTACHMENT IS THE CAUSE OF CONFUSION

Lord Krishna helps Arjuna to discern the true cause of suffering. "those who are deeply attached to pleasure and worldly power cannot attain the determinate intellect concentrated on God" (2:44). Krishna clearly instructs Arjuna saying, "Your right is to work only, but never to the fruit thereof. Be not instrumental in making your actions bear fruit, nor let your attachment be to inaction. Arjuna, perform your duties established in yoga, renouncing attachment, and even-temperament in success and failure; evenness of temper is called yoga"; (2:47-48). For a person who has attained equanimity, even the scriptures are useless. Krishna makes a most daring statement that; A Brahman, who has attained enlightenment, has the same use of all the Vedas as one who stands at the brink of the sheet of water overflowing on all sides has for a small reservoir of water (2:46).He assures Arjuna that, "he who has given up all desires and move free from attachment, egoism and thirst for enjoyment attains peace" (2:71).

3) BE YOGI -THE ROYAL PATH TO DISCERNMENT

In an attempt to lead him to the royal path of discernment, Krishna says to Arjuna: "He who acts offering all actions to God, and shaking off attachment, remains untouched by sin, as the lotus leaf by water"; (5:10).The wise look with the same eye on a Brahman endowed with learning and culture, a cow, an elephant, dog, and a pariah too (5:18). According to Krishna, when the disciplined mind of a person is firmly established in God and is actively engaged in the service of all beings, it attains Brahma, who is all peace (5:25). He will be in a position to regard stone, earth and gold alike (6:8): Arjuna, he who looks on all as one, on the analogy of his own self, and looks upon the joy and sorrow of all with a similar eye, - such a yogi is deemed the highest of all (6:32).The awareness that all beings have emerged from the same source and their destination is also the same will enable one to overcome one's irrational responses of attachment and aversion (7:6). Krishna offers Arjuna an easy way to reach this state of equilibrium through *bhakti* (devotion) and says, "Arjuna, whatever you do, whatever you eat, whatever you offer as oblation to the sacred fire, whatever you bestow as a gift, whatever you do by way of penance, offer it all to me (9:27). As a powerful means to convince his beloved disciple, Krishna is transfigured in front of Arjuna and reveals his glorious divine form with an effulgence of a thousand suns where he could see the universe, its past, present and future, gods and goddesses, even the terrible conclusion of the battle they are about to wage and the looming mass destruction. Krishna reveals himself as the embodiment of Time *(kala)* and warns him: "Even without you all these warriors arrayed in the enemy's camp must die. These warriors stand already slain by me; be you only an instrument, Arjuna. Do you kill Drona, and Bhishma, Jayadratha and Karna and even other brave warriors; who stand already killed by me; fear not. You will surely conquer the enemies in this war; therefore, fight"; (11:32-34).

4) TRANSCENDMENT ABOVE GUNAS

When a person is capable of watching everything that happens within and around him dispassionately and acting with an attitude of detachment, s/he has reached *sthithaprajna* (equanimity) and attained *Samadhi* (liberation). When light and discernment dawn in this body, as well as in the mind and senses. (14:11),one will be free from every turbulence of mind and body. He who sitting like a witness, is not disturbed by *gunas,* and who, knowing that the *gunas* alone move among *gunas,* remains established in identity with God, and never falls off from that state (14:23).

Krishna's final warning is even more authoritative: "If taking your stand on egoism, you think, 'I will not fight', vain is this resolve of yours; nature will drive you to the act. That action too which you are not willing to undertake through ignorance, - bound by your own duty born of your nature, you will helplessly perform." (18:59-60). After his extensive and magnificent discourse on discernment, Krishna leaves everything to the discretion of Arjuna saying: "Thus has this wisdom, more secret than secrecy itself, been imparted to you by me. Fully pondering it, do as you like" (18:63). Being fully enlightened, Arjuna responds: "Krishna, by your grace my delusion has fled and wisdom has been gained by me. I stand shorn of all doubts. I will do your bidding". (18:73). At last, a happy ending to a long walk to discernment.

4.1.2 Lessons to be learnt from Shri Arjun:

1) Immense faith in God
2) Applied ultimate passion always and everywhere
3) Always indulged in learning from competition

4) Intense focused with unwandering concentration
5) Patience and Perseverance in hard work
6) Conundrum before taking feasible solution
7) Loyal towards duty
8) Brave and Fearless

4.2.1 Lessons FROM HANUMAN – HERO OF SUNDARKAND – (ALWAYS IN ACTION)

Shri Hanuman had always illustrated the symbol of strength. We have to realize whether our strength is made aware by our act or by others. In other words, one's entity is recognized by their work and character. During the acid test, one needs to overcome the obstacle with challenging propaganda. Apart from this even patience and perservance is essential with almighty's divine blessing. It doesn't matter who works from the beginning but how differently one works till the end. One can't measure the length or magnitude of fight. A warrior though might get wounded but will never give up or flee in between but fight till the end. Do not concede the defeat but be determined to win the journey of fight. Do not fear to face the unexpected Brahmmastra with stern determination. The realm of the unknown which are unknowns has to be encountered with smart trailor-made trade-offs. Obviously there should be many alternatives designed at initial stage itself as per the motive and objective of the goal/venture. For this one has to believe in –

➢ Power of possibilities
➢ The strength of being flexible
➢ Support coming from unexpected quarters
➢ Alertness to recognize and leverage
➢ Surfacing of the hidden strengths at early stage
➢ On the spot Assessment of facts
➢ Keeping the larger mission in mind
➢ Remembering back the needs

Hanuman illustrated the above actions which were consistently in action towards the goal of bringing back Sita from unknown location. He was successful in accomplishing this task within 3 years and this incident of eloping of Sita happened in the 10th year of the exile of

Lord Ram. Remember, greatness comes when you work in tandem for the betterment of yourself and others. Your accomplishments might bring joy, but helping others brings renown.

4.2.2 Lessons to be Learnt from Hanuman:

1. High Aim:

A fascinating story states that, when Hanuman was a child, he leaped into the sky thinking that the sun was a large ripe mango. To grab and relish the fruit in the sky, Hanuman grew larger and larger and swallowed the sun. Indra shot him down. Vayu, the Lord of wind, who is also known as Hanuman's spiritual father, got very upset. He emptied the universe of wind, and all the creatures started dying. Hanuman was not only revived but also granted eternal life.

Thus, aim for a higher goal, and the universe will work its way out for you.

2. Symbol of strength and energy:

Ramayana is an evidence of Hanuman's strength. He alone dared to leap across the ocean and get into Lanka. When Lakshman needed to be revived, Hanuman flew to the Kailash Parvat seeking Sanjeevani plant. Many stories illustrate the umpteen strength and bravery of our Veer Hanuman. So, if you want to be successful, **have faith in your capabilities and be brave to take decisions that are out of your comfort zone**. Hanuman embodied fearlessness better than any other modern superheroes. He took decisions, risks, came past negative experiences and gave his best fearlessly.

3. Loyalty:

Lord Hanuman was a loyal friend to one and all. He helped Sugreev seek Lord Rama's help to win his kingdom back from Vali. He assisted and helped Lord Rama with unflinching loyalty in every way possible. He gained love of the Lord.

4. Selfless devotion:

After meeting Rama, Hanuman found a higher purpose in life. Rama's journey became his mission, and he worked towards it tirelessly, without any selfish motive. Just like the other superheroes, it is his contribution to more significant things that gave him a special place in our hearts.

5. Adaptability:

One of the fantastic superpowers of Hanuman was his ability to adapt. Within seconds he could turn into an ant, grow as big as a mountain, travel by land, sea or air, travel faster than the gusting wind or higher than a bird. He overcame all the hurdles with limitless power and flexibility. In our lives too, we need to be adaptable in the same way. We should develop the habit of looking at the things in details, growing large to get a holistic view and settle our ego to find solutions. Through speed, agility, and will-power we can sail through worst situations unharmed.

6. Always say "Yes Sir":

As mentioned above, Hanuman was a great manager. He believed in teamwork and at the same time never entertained any excuses. From getting into Ravana's abode and meeting Sita single-handedly, to building a bridge over the ocean – Hanuman did it all, without giving lame excuses.

To accomplish your goals, stay focused and stop giving excuses!

7. Dynamism:

Lord Hanuman was dynamic and multi-faceted. He conquered immortality and could achieve any feat with ease. Once, when Rama and Lakshmana were kidnapped by Ahiravana and taken to Patala loka, Hanuman went to their rescue. There he realized that to vanquish Ahiravana he must extinguish five lamps in North, South, East, West, and Upward directions. At that point, Hanuman took a five-faced form. This shows how dynamic he was. In a normal life scenario, open your mind to learning, challenge yourself, stay on your toes and welcome success and failure with stride.

8. Good Listener:

Hanuman was a great listener. It is due to this patience and good listening qualities he was able to guide and show people the right path. For example, his advice to Vibhishan helped him conquer

Lanka. Keep in mind, that unless you listen correctly, you won't be able to give solutions.

9. Never Give up:

All superheroes and most importantly our original superhero – Hanuman teaches us to never give up. He never shied away from responsibilities, took charge and fulfilled all his commitments. To him nothing was impossible.

10. Always in Action(Quality of Leadership):

Don't be an escapist but lead from the front. Even during the worst crisis, a leader will always stand in front of his/her team and guide them towards victory.

4.3 Lessons From Ravana:

- Divine faith
- Very scholarly King
- Great strategist
- Have humility to withdrew when it is still in your favour
- Learn from negative consequences
- High embraced listening skills
- Determination of achieving
- Stubborn attitude – is not acceptable
- Very arrogant behavior

4.4 Checklists from Knowledge base of Vyasa as below:

1) Action of Actors for retaining the Relationship
2) Literacy of Innovation –
a) Navigate through unknown
b) Formulate many alternatives so that in case of failure – it can be implemented.
c) Complimenting Link
d) Always correct the Slices
3) Work Commitment - Golden chain for enrichment
a) Shravan –Consistent hard work

b) Pathan – Reading and preaching scriptures
c) Abhyas & Manan – Thoughtful, Meditate, reverence and practice regularly
d) Chintan – Reflecting the thoughts of what you need to preach
e) Kathan – Achieving the success and feeling enlightened about it.

4) Summarization of above Winning formulas :
a) Arise, awake and stop not till the goal is reached
b) Work, Work, Work that you preach about and let this be your motive
c) Bless your mistakes. If you fail a thousand times, make the attempt once more
d) Stop running and face the brutes
e) Faith, faith, faith in yourself
f) Blame more for your own faults
g) Let the heart be followed whenever there is conflict between the brain and heart
h) Full attention and no tension
i) Service to humanity is service to God
j) Strength is the only thing which we require in this life

5) Some of fluent management strategies to enhance the overall efficiency and values of skill:
a) Awareness
b) Understanding Unlearning -
c) Grouping v/s Arrangements.
d) Change v/s Transformation.
e) Interesting v/s Important things.
f) Profit Equation.
g) Performance of Appraisal.
h) Efficiency v/s Effectiveness.
i) Seven pointers to success.

a) **Awareness:** The quality of being in state to acquire the Knowledge and have better understating of the things around.

Example: One must be aware about the things happening in the company and at the work place.

b) **Understanding Unlearning:** One needs to discard the things learnt before. (Especially outdated information and habits)

Example: In Company we should unlearn things which are not useful.

c) **Grouping v/s Arrangements:** Grouping refers to set of people come together to act on the things assigned. Arrangements are the plans to group people as team in the organization.

Example: Grouping and Arrangements are done in Corporate to bring gender equality and mutual respect for each other in the team.

d) **Change v/s Transformation:** Change is to modify or alter that are the impact of External sources ex- Climate change, Change in state of Ice cube into water due to heat. Transformation Completely change and it is a complex and painful procedure it is an impact of internal sources. caterpillar to a butterfly is a very lengthy and complex process.

Example: A candidate who has changed according to the education he/she had till now, and it's time to transform into a ready professional to work for a corporate house.

e) **Interesting v/s important things:** Interesting things are the things which keep us curious and hold our attention. Important things are which have great value.

Example: One who is interested in watching blogs on the internet during office hours must trade off and focus on the important things assigned to him/her.

f) **Profit equation:** Every company exist with the primary objective of earning profits so the company emphasis on the profit maximization

Profit = Revenue – Cost incurred.

Example: Each one of us working for the company are a cost element to the company as they pay us the salary.

g)   Performance Appraisal: It is a review of an employee's performance and his contribution to the Company.

Example: The better we perform and meet the expectations, Higher the chance to climb upwards in the Management hierarchy. (Promotion, salary hike etc.)

h)   Effectiveness v/s Efficient: Effectiveness refers to produce the intended result. Efficient refers to achieving maximum result in less time.

Example: In a company one needs to be Efficient.

i)   Seven pointers to Success:

i. Shun catastrophizing and prepare for the worst

ii. Developing Autonomy to be disciplined

iii. Freeing Interpersonal Relations which should be aloof from moha

iv. Need for Achievement should be the objective

v. Success role modeling at planning stage itself

vi. Purpose is the ultimate achievable goal

vii. Integrity towards the goal with knowledge and emotional intelligence

Life Skills For Ethical Sustainable Corporate Life

5.1 IMPORTANCE

Ethics is a judgmental choice as to how to behave in one's life which includes a knowledge base, skills, and attitude. Everyone of us need to choose our own way life based on our chosen values of life. In making such a choice we should look around to the different models and decide to choose a model appropriate to us. It is conscientious decision arising out of our awakened conscious. To lead an ethical life we need appropriate life skills. To discuss these skills is the purpose of the lecture.

1) **Analytical Outlook:**

We should keenly observe how different behave in life and what are their consequences and through that process decide what should be our way of life.

2) **Clear Goal of Life:**

We should be clear as to who we are, why we here and what are we going to do about our life? We should define how this opportunity should be utilized. There are people who are alive even today though they died long back. There are people who are dead though they are alive. This defines clear purpose of Life.

3) **Simplicity:**

Simplicity is a hallmark of great men and women. They are simple in their dress, food and way of life. If we decide to be simple and modest and do not dream of any luxuries of life we can utilize our wholelife for upliftment of society, improving the mankind. Such people who dedicate themselves to progress of society and mankind live forever. In essence we should not utilize this life to make over personal life beautiful but make the society and mankind more beautiful. Those who live for others really live. Others are moving towards death slowly. Death is loss of values of life, Life is a life of values. We are human beings and we should come out of animalistic passions.

4) Concern for our Clean Image:

We should have a clean image in whatever profession we choose as well as in private life. We should not do anything that is not worthy of our education and upbringing and set new standards of behavior for people to follow.

5) Faith in the Almighty God:

We definitely know that we are not the creation of this world. Our creator who also maintain this world has certain universal rules if followed we will become decline. These golden rules consist of :

- Commitment to duty or profession
- Commitment to Society
- Commitment to excel in whatever we do
- Commitment to show path to them as to how live better.

This way we should develop life skills to live within our means, give out more than we receive and not aspire to create wealth, but aspire to create strong character.

5.2 Capsules mentioned in Bhagwad Gita

Gita tells us how to get out of this universal phenomenon by prescribing the following capsules:

- Cultivate sound philosophy of life.
- Identify with inner core of self-sufficiency.
- Get out of the habitual mindset towards the pairs of opposites.
- Strive for excellence through work is worship.
- Build up an internal integrated reference point to face impulses and emotions.
- Pursue ethico-moral rectitude.

Cultivating this understanding by a manager would lead him to emancipation from falsifying ego-conscious state of confusion and distortion, to a state of pure and free mind i.e. universal, supreme consciousness wherefrom he can prove his effectiveness in discharging whatever duties that have fallen to his domain.

Bhagawan's advice is relevant here:

"tasmaatsarveshukaaleshumamanusmarahyuddha cha" that states that under all circumstances remember Me and then fight' (Fight means perform your duties). Whatever the excellent and best ones do, the commoners follow, so says Lord Krishna in the Gita. In one verse the Lord says " I, do not need to work, yet I am working continuously, because if I stop working, everybody would do the same, resulting in total chaos", This is the leadership quality prescribed in the Gita. The visionary leader must also be a missionary, extremely practical, intensively dynamic and capable of translating dreams into reality. This dynamism and strength of a true leader flows from an inspired and spontaneous motivation to help others. "I am the strength of those who are devoid of personal desire and attachment. O Arjuna, I am the legitimate desire in those, who are not opposed to righteousness" says Sri Krishna in the 10th Chapter of the Gita.

5.3 The Ultimate Message of Gita for Managers

The despondent position of Arjuna in the first chapter of the Gita is a typical human situation which may come in the life of all men of action some time or other. Sri Krishna by sheer power of his inspiring words raised the level of Arjuna's mind from the state of inertia to the state of righteous action, from the state of faithlessness to the state of faith and self-confidence in the ultimate victory of Dharma(ethical action). They are the powerful words of courage of strength, of self-confidence, of faith in one's own infinite power, of the glory, of valour in the life of active people and of the need for intense calmness in the midst of intense action.

When Arjuna got over his despondency and stood ready to fight, Sri Krishna gave him the gospel for using his spirit of intense action not for his own benefit, not for satisfying his own greed and desire, but for using his action for the good of many, with faith in the ultimate victory of ethics over unethical actions and truth over untruth. Arjuna responds by emphatically declaring that all his delusions were removed and that he is ready to do what is expected of him in the given situation.

Sri Krishna's advice with regard to temporary failures in actions is 'No doer of good ever ends in misery'. Every action should produce results: good action produces good results and evil begets nothing but evil. Therefore always act well and be rewarded.

And finally the Gita's consoling message for all men of action is: He who follows My ideal in all walks of life without losing faith in the ideal or never deviating from it, I provide him with all that he needs (Yoga) and protect what he has already got (Kshema).

Reference

A.C. Bhaktivedanta Swami Prabhupada, *Bhagavad-gita; As it is* (Macmillan Edition), The Bhaktivedanta Book Trust, 2012.

John C Maxwell, *How Successful people grow; 15ways to get ahead in life*, Center Street, 2012.

E. R. Thompson, *Secrets of success*.

Michael A. Singer, *The Untethered Soul*, New Harbinger Publication, Inc., 2007

James Clear, *The Psychology of Money; Timeless lessons on wealth, greed, and happiness*, Jaico Publishing House, 2020.

Shiv Khera, *You Can Win*, Macmillan Indian Ltd., 1998

A R K Sharma, *Swami Vivekananda's Winning Formulas to become Successful Managers*, Sri Sarada Book House, 2011

Chatufwedi, B. 2006. *The Mahabharata: An inquiry in the human condition*. New Delhi: Orient Longman.   [Links]

Frein, B. 2012. Fundamentalism and narrative approaches to the Gospels. *Biblical Theology Bulletin* 22:12-18.   [Links]

Gandhi, M.K. [s.a.] *Influence of Bhagavad Gita*. [Online.] Retrieved from: http://en.wikipedia.org/wiki/Influence_of_Bhagavad_Gita [20 November 2012].   [Links]

Ganguli, K.M. [s.a.] *Mahabharata of Vyasa*. [Online.]Retrieved from: www.mahabharataonline.com/translation/mahabharata_01002.php. [20 November 2012].   [Links]

Griffith, R.T.H. [s.a.] *Rigveda*. [Online.] Retrieved from: http://www.sacred-texts.com/hin/rigveda/index.htm [20 November 2012].   [Links]

Guruparananda, S. [s.a.] *Katha Upanishad*. [Online.] Retrieved from: http://archive.org/details/KathaUpanishad [20 November 2012].   [Links]

Güyandaka, J. 1994. *The Bhagavad-Gita or The Song Divine.* Gorakhpur: GovindBhavanKaryalaya. [Links]

Kaji, D.S. 2001. *Common sense about uncommon wisdom: Ancient teachings of Vedanta.* Honesdale: The Himalayan Institute Press. [Links]

Knapp, S. [s.a.] *Vedic Culture/Hinduism: A short introduction.* [Online.] Retrieved from: www.stephen-knapp.com/vedic_culture_hinduism_a_short_introduction.htm [20 November 2012]. [Links]

Krishnananda, S. [s.a.] *Mundakopanishad.* [Online.] Retrieved from: http://www.swami-krishnananda.org/mundaka_0.html [20 November 2012]. [Links]

Nadumuri, J. 2010. *Bharatha.* [Online.] Retrieved from: http://ancientvoice.wikidot.com/mbh:bharata [20 November 2012]. [Links]

Nikhilananda, S. [s.a.] *The Gospel of Sri Ramakrishna.* [Online.] Retrieved from: www.belurmath.org/gospel/index.htm [20 November 2012]. [Links]

Ramacharaka, Y. 2010. *The Bhagavad Gita's teachings on spiritual discernment.* Whitefish: Kessinger Publishing. [Links]

Wikipedia [s.a.] *Mahabharata.* [Online.] Retrieved from: http://en.wikipedia.org/wiki/Mahabharata [20 November 2012]. [Links]

http://www.scielo.org.za/scielo.php?script=sci_arttext&pid=S1015-87582013000300015

K. Perumpallikunnel, Acta theol. vol.33 suppl.17 Bloemfontein Nov. 2013

https://journalppw.com/index.php/jpsp/article/view/13965

About the Author

Dr. Veda D. Malagatti

Dr. Veda D. Malagatti is a faculty in a management institution. Her vision has in-depth knowledge of research in the field of management as she has pursued Doctorate of Philosophy in Management from Karnataka Univeristy, Karnataka State, India and she hails from Mumbai. She has degree of management, Cost Management Accountant- Intermediate, and NET eligibility. She has both industry and teaching experience. She has total 23 papers either published or presented in international / national journal and international conference proceedings. She is also author for a book titled "Costing in Service Industry" by Cambridgescholar publishing, U.K.. She is Member of Editorial Board for IIP proceedings and has worked as editor for two books. She has keen interest in enriching knowledge in 360 degree with persistence and perservance. She believes in 3P's namely persistence, perservance and perfection with ethics to lead suceessfully.

www.ingramcontent.com/pod-product-compliance
Lightning Source LLC
LaVergne TN
LVHW041633070526
838199LV00052B/3331